Decoupage

Decoupage

A practical, step-by-step guide

Tracy Boomer &
Deborah Morbin

METZ PRESS

Dedication

For our children: Natasha, Alexander, Sophie and James:
You can do anything if you try.

Authors' acknowledgements

Some people (our husbands) laughed when we told them we were going to write a book on decoupage. However, they did become very supportive when they realised we were serious and, as husbands, tend to do, offered all sorts of suggestions - most of which we ignored completely! So thank you, Geoff and Christopher, for helping with the children and keeping the home fires burning while we were busy. Also, a big thank you to Christopher for his help with the spelling, punctuation and text, we all knew that irritating Virgo nit-picking would come in useful one day!

There were other people whom we approached about our book who didn't laugh. In fact, some were so enthusiastic and helpful that they deserve a special mention. They are Wilsia Metz, our publisher and editor, who believed in us from the beginning, whose wicked sense of humour and consummate professionalism inspired us to go the extra mile; David Pickett, our incredibly talented photographer, who handled all interference with a smile; Chris Rayner and Joan Launspach of Brasch Hobby (Heritage) for their advice and free samples; Adri Franck Perring for the nautical illustrations on pages 64-65; Roger Armitage of McCalls Patterns for the Wallies brochures he sent us; Lella Kondylia from the Handpainted Transfer Company for all the transfers sent at such short notice;

Penny Johnston for the use of her beautiful house during a very long photo shoot; Bitou Crafts of Knysna for props; Carrie de Beer and Amanda Cloete for helping us at the eleventh hour with cutting; and Graham Chalmers (the lawyer with a heart) for sound legal and marketing advice (and oysters).

We would also like to thank the following Paper Companies for their good wishes and giving us the go-ahead to use and display their papers: Henry Porter of Porter Designs, Bath, England. Conrad H Nagle of Lloyd Johnson Card Distributions, Randburg, SA for Grafiche Tassotti papers. Petter Carlmark of Finmark, Australia.

Your quick response was greatly appreciated and we hope that your sales increase because of this book.

Also, thanks to Brasch Hobby, Plascon and Pratley for allowing us to name and photograph their products.

Last, but certainly not least, thank you June Bisschop for teaching us this wonderful craft so many years ago and becoming a special friend in the process.

M ETZ
PRESS

Published by Metz Press
Unit 106, Hoheizen Park 1,
Hoheizen Avenue,
Hoheizen 7530 South Africa

First edition June 2001
Second imprint October 2001
Copyright © Metz Press
Text copyright © Tracy Boomer & Deborah Morbin
Photographs © Metz Press

EDITOR	Wilsia Metz
DESIGN CONCEPT	Mandy McKay
PAGE LAY-OUT	Lindie Metz
LAY-OUT CONSULTANT	Gerhardt van Rooyen
PHOTOGRAPHY	Alchemy Foto Imaging cc, Cape Town
PRODUCTION	Andrew de Kock
REPRODUCTION	Cape Imaging Bureau, Cape Town
PRINTING AND BINDING	Tien Wah Press, Singapore
ISBN	1-875001-15-8

Contents

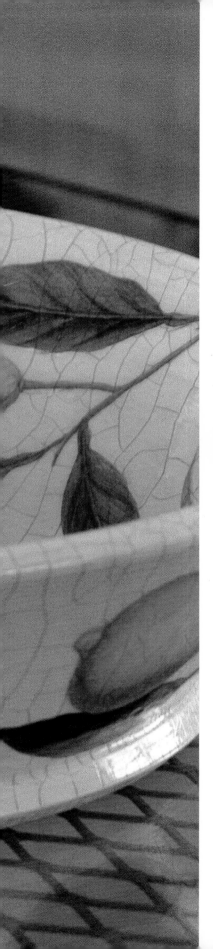

Introduction

A few years ago, having both moved to Knysna, we enrolled in a course together to learn a new craft. Little did we know that this hobby would prove to be so pleasurable and satisfying that it would lead our lives in a new direction. Our children were very young at the time and the course was like a breath of fresh air compared to the daily routine of nappies, bottles and night-feeds. We were very lucky to have as our tutor one of South Africa's leading

'decoupeurs', a master craftsman named June Bisschop, who has sadly now retired from teaching. We both looked forward to those lessons, not only to get away from the kids for a morning, but because of their therapeutic quality and the fact that we were creating something beautiful without having to be able to draw or paint.

June took us through the basics, teaching us the traditional form of decoupage using 40 layers of varnish to 'bury' the print! This may sound rather daunting but, given today's quick-drying varnishes, it's really not too bad. Learning to do the craft properly from the beginning gave us the foundations from which we have progressed to experiment and to understand what can and can't be done with the various types of varnishes and paints available in this country. It did not take us too long to find the short cuts, which are necessary when you make a lot of items or need to make a gift in a hurry.

To be perfectly honest, we don't use the traditional form that often anymore, except for really special items. But when we do, there is nothing that can beat the finish, which ends up looking something like French polish.

After completing the course, a group of us continued to meet regularly to practise our new 'art'. People came and went but we were the diehard decoupeurs who attended religiously, experimenting continuously and then sharing what we'd taught ourselves with our fellow crafters. We began taking orders and supplying shops. As our work became noticed, people began to approach us to give them lessons. We found that some of our students had already done courses but had not understood them sufficiently to practise with confidence. We therefore tried to make the lessons as simple and straightforward as possible, once again always going back to the basics.

Our exhibition at the Nederburg Arts Festival in 1999 led to greater exposure and more students. However, we found that more and more of our time was being spent answering queries on decoupage from people in towns we'd never even heard of – and we still don't know how they found our numbers! We began to realize that it would be far easier on both ourselves and people telephoning us for advice if we had printed notes to give them. That is why we have embarked on this project. We hope that you'll find the book informative and easy to follow. We also hope that it will help to bring out the artist in you and lead to many happy hours of decoupaging.

About decoupage

The term 'decoupage' comes from the French word, *decouper*, meaning 'to cut out'. It refers to the art of cutting, arranging and gluing pictures to a surface to create a whole new composition. Finally, it is sealed with layers of varnish to 'bury' the picture.

A form of decoupage was practised in ancient times by the Chinese who used vividly-coloured paper cutouts to decorate windows, lanterns, boxes and other items. But it is oriental lacquer work from the late 1700s that we associate most closely with today's decoupage. Intricately decorated and lacquered furniture brought back by traders from China and Japan became so popular in Europe that demand soon outstripped supply. So enterprising Italian cabinet-makers began cutting, gluing and varnishing to produce fake lacquer work to keep up with the demand. This became known as *lacca contrafatta*, or counterfeit lacquer. At around the same time, European royalty and nobility began commissioning master-painters to decorate their furniture, walls and ceilings. The poorer classes could not afford this extravagance, and resorted to colouring and cutting out artists' drawings, then gluing and varnishing

them to create the same effect. So decoupage became known as *l'arte del povero*, or 'poor man's art'. Funnily enough, and much to the masters' dismay, it became more popular than the real thing!

By far the most popular story regarding decoupage is that the ladies of the French Court, including the infamous Marie Antoinette, practised it. Apparently they practised their hobby with such a degree of enthusiasm that they cut up original artwork and used these cut-outs to decorate bookshelves, cabinets, fans, hatboxes and other items of furniture.

At the time of the French Revolution, Decoupage Guilds which were formed all over Europe and had been going strongly for many years, disbanded and decoupage almost became a lost art.

A small number of devoted craftsmen passed on their knowledge to their own children and grandchildren, though, and decoupage experienced a revival in the early 1900s. Embossed papers and braids were incorporated into many designs, and the style became more florid and sentimental, with lots of overlapping collages.

It is hardly surprising that a craft with such a long and fascinating history is experiencing yet another enthusiastic revival. Over time anyone who pursues this craft can progress from making simple items to turning out works as beautiful and creative as those produced by the ladies of the French court – and technology has made it possible to do so without cutting up precious original artwork.

About this book

This book is based on our teaching approach, which has proved to be successful in the past. Instead of describing specific projects step by step throughout, we give you step-by-step instructions for the basic techniques which you can apply to decoupage any item of your choice. If you know how to prepare specific base materials and achieve specific decoupage finishes, you can explore the limitless possibilities of this popular craft to your heart's content and transform anything into a decorative object or special gift.

Wherever possible, we've tried not to be too boringly technical, *but please read all the instructions*. This will enable you to avoid all the many expensive and time-wasting mistakes we have made through a long process of trial and error.

You should find all the products needed to create beautiful decoupage from your local hardware store and craft shop. If you find it difficult to obtain any product, please consult the list of suppliers on page 108. Many of these suppliers offer a mail-order service and will gladly arrange for products to be forwarded to wherever you are. We have suggested specific products because these are the ones that we have tried and tested. We felt that by being either too vague and general, or giving too many alternatives, we may confuse you.

If you cannot find the specific products we list, bear in mind that there are others available which can also be used. Ask your local hardware store or craft shop to advise you or to suggest alternatives.

Getting started

In this chapter we discuss what you will need to tackle your first decoupage project. Wherever possible we have tried to give you all the options available. There are some purchases that you will only need to make once, for instance the tools required. Look after these, keep them clean and away from spouses and children and they will last a long time.

 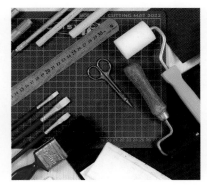

When people think of decoupage, wooden boxes always seem to spring to mind. But there are lots of options available which we've covered in this chapter. Don't stop here – use your imagination and experiment with a variety of base materials. It has been our experience that what most people find daunting is the large choice of varnishes available on the market. We have simplified this for you by discussing the varnishes that we know and prefer to use.

Don't rush out and buy all these varnishes at once. Try them out gradually and find the ones that work best for you. It has taken us years to get around to using all of these products, so don't be in a hurry. Remember, the key word when it comes to decoupage, is patience.

Finally, don't be tempted to skim over this chapter because we have included many useful tips and ideas.

Papers and prints

ABOVE *These sheets of wrapping paper are all suitable for either cut-outs as used on the toy box below, or complete covering.*

A wide variety of source papers and prints is available to work with – your choice is really unlimited.

Gift wrap

The most popular and cheapest source of pictures is wrapping paper. The range available today is varied and of such good quality that it is tempting to look no further. Once you start using it for decoupage, wrapping paper will take on a new meaning in your life – never again will you be able to walk past a sheet of paper without giving it a long, hard look. Presents will be neatly opened so that you can reuse the gift wrap.

The quality of paper is important, as thicker paper is easier to work with. But don't rule out thinner paper, as experience will enable you to overcome the problems that it presents. Tissue paper can be used but is difficult to work with and requires extra sealing. Try to avoid wrapping paper coated in wax; we've found that it's not suitable since the varnish with which you have to seal the paper before cutting out the images, does not adhere.

Magazines and photographs

A question frequently asked is whether photographs can be used. Although this is a wonderful way of personalizing a gift for someone, don't use the original photograph.

The varnishes used are likely to react horribly with the chemicals in the photographs. To overcome this, use a photocopy of the photograph. The same applies to magazine pictures and newspaper cuttings, as the print on the reverse side tends to show through.

Photocopies

What would we do without the modern technology of a colour copier! It allows you to make copies of your favourite picture without having to destroy the original.

You have the freedom to enlarge, reduce, change the colour of your picture or create mirror images. And don't forget about ordinary traditional black and white photocopies – they are cheaper and can be very striking. Bear in mind that photocopies often come out darker than the original – you may want to adjust the photocopier to produce a lighter print. Photocopies can also be stained to give them an aged look (see Tea staining, page 43).

Computer-generated pictures

Another question frequently asked is whether computer-generated pictures can be used. It all depends on the printer used to make a print-out of the picture. If the picture has been printed on an ink-jet printer, it cannot be used, but you should be able to use pictures printed on a laser printer.

A good way of testing whether a picture was printed on an inkjet or a laser printer, is to wet your finger and run it over the picture. If it smudges, it was printed on an inkjet printer and cannot be used. Unfortunately most people have ink-jet printers for home use. But once again, a photocopy of the original picture is a way of overcoming this.

BELOW *A perfect, personalised gift for granny, mom or a teen-age daughter. This all-purpose box was decorated with pictures of a child taken from birth to present day. We used a digital photocopier to make copies of the photographs (which were all colour originally), which we tea-stained and hand-coloured with watered-down acrylic paint in certain areas.*

Transfers

Using transfers in decoupage is not strictly true decoupage but a little bit of cheating to make things easier has never hurt anyone. You can either buy ready-made transfers (see list of suppliers, page 108), or make your own as described below. By applying Heritage Transfer Glaze on top of your picture, you end up with a thin, pliable piece of 'plastic' – very similar in texture to cling-wrap. The advantage of transfers is that you don't need as many coats of varnish to bury it because the picture is so thin. It is also easier to apply to a curved surface (such as an ostrich egg or a ceramic or clay pot). The Chinese lettering on the writing set below would have been difficult to cut out, so we made transfers instead. Transfers are also an ideal way of putting other writ-

Making your own transfers

- Cut out your print and apply at least 6 coats of transfer glaze in opposite directions (side-to-side, top-to-bottom). Allow to dry after every coat.

- When the picture is dry, soak it in water for approximately 30 minutes. Leave it in the water and begin rubbing gently on the paper at the back of the print until it eventually all comes off. What's left will be a thin, flexible transfer.

- A little trick we have learned is to take the transfer directly from the water and roll it straight onto the item to be decoupaged. It doesn't need gluing, as it is sticky when wet. Ideally, the picture that you choose to make a transfer of should not have delicately cut out parts, as the rubbing may cause pieces to tear or break off.

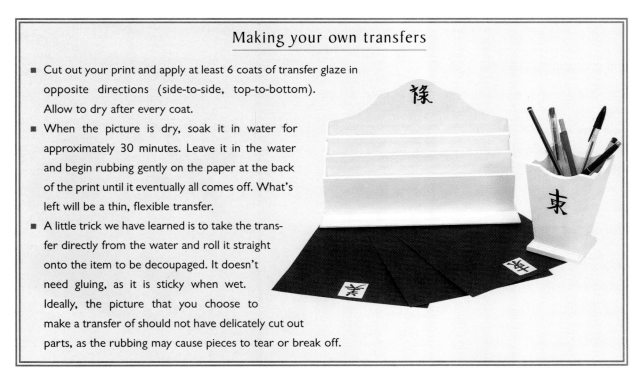

ing or company logos onto your work. Cut around the entire logo, leaving about 2 mm all round.

We've found that transfers work better on a light background rather than a very dark one, as colour intensity is lost.

Cards, prints and 'Wallies'

There is a large variety of cards and prints available, which can be used in decoupage. They are usually available from framing shops. Some decoupage and craft shops also have a good selection. Always be mindful of copyright laws, which exist on many of these prints.

Wallies provide you with a large and varied range of pictures that you won't find anywhere else. A Wallie is a pre-pasted, vinyl-coated cut-out. You will find them at your local hardware shop, craft shops and some interior decorating shops – if they don't have any, ask them to order some.

Wallies make life easier since they take the 'coup' out of decoupage because you don't have to cut! You don't have to glue either because they are pre-pasted (see pages 100–101 for detailed instructions on how to use them to decorate a toy box).

Copyright

As mentioned above, copyright exists on numerous prints, wrapping paper designs and pictures in books. We feel that if you've bought a print or a sheet of wrapping paper, you may use it in any way that you choose. But you may not make copies of prints, wrapping paper, or any printed material, to sell. Also proceed with caution when you use these images to make items to sell.

Keep in mind that certain famous cartoon characters – and we're probably not even allowed to mention their names here – have such strict copyright laws attached to them that you could end up in court should you be accused of infringing these.

There are copyright-free books available and you are allowed to copy images from these books for personal use, not commercially.

BELOW *This planter had been standing outside, unused, for about six years and was a real challenge to decorate. We used calico as a base colour and painted the rim the same dark green as the inside. A yellow-ochre wash was applied over the calico and then the pot was antiqued. The Wallie was trimmed down and rearranged to fit onto the pot; the project was completed with 6 coats of oil-based varnish. The yellow tinge from the varnish enhances the effect that we wanted to achieve with the antiquing.*

Don't be intimidated by the size of something like this – we made it in two days and the compliments keep rolling in!

Base materials

Your options here really are boundless. For the enthusiastic decoupeur the sky is the limit and if we could get up there, we would probably decoupage that as well! Almost any surface can be decorated no matter how large or small.

Old wood

Old frames, boxes, furniture, basically anything can be decorated. Old pieces with a highly lacquered or polished surface would need a lot of preparation, though. This involves wiping down the item with spirits to remove any wax or grease. When dry, you would then have to sand it with coarse-grain sandpaper, followed by another sanding with a finer-grade paper. Only once the surface is smooth and free of anything sticky or flaking will you be able to work on it.

New wood/superwood

There is a large and varied selection of wooden products available for decoupage. By far the most popular and easily available are the so-called new wood or superwood products.

This is a man-made, medium-density fibre product and is relatively unaffected by humidity, which means it will not shrink or swell with time. It is also the easiest to work with as well as being inexpensive.

Ceramics

Ceramics sold for use in decoupage are normally bisque-fired without any further treatment or finishing. There is a large variety available but bear in mind that the items you make will be purely decorative. Since a bowl can be wiped clean with a wet cloth but not washed in warm, soapy water, it can only be used for fruit or other dry items.

Not many people attempt to work with ceramics, but don't be put off, as it is really very rewarding. It is possible to

BELOW A selection of decoupage blanks: galvanized steel buckets, bisque-fired ceramic jar, glass jar, clay flower-pot and several new-wood items, including a picture frame. These ordinary-looking items can all be transformed into beautiful decorative items and gifts by following the instructions in Decoupage finishes on pages 51–83.

work on glazed pottery or china but over time the varnish and pictures will inevitably flake off so it's not really worth it.

Glass

Plates, coasters and jugs are amongst the glass items that can be decoupaged. Like the bisque ceramics this is also purely decorative, only more so because scratching will lift the paint from the glass. Once again, the area that you have worked on can only be wiped clean but not be submerged in hot, soapy water.

Galvanized steel

There are a lot of galvanized steel products (buckets, watering cans, bowls, vases and so on) currently available on the market. They are inexpensive and make beautiful gifts, but are often under-utilised by decoupeurs. A little more preparation

is involved to combat rust and to ensure adhesion of the base coats of paint, but the end product makes it worth the effort.

Walls and floors

Redecorating a room by using the decoupage techniques that you have learnt will be a wonderful challenge. And don't worry – you don't always have to use 40 coats of varnish!

You can decorate any wall with a smooth finish, as well as wooden floors (which unfortunately would need a thorough sanding first) with cut-outs or the Wallies we mentioned earlier. The range of Wallies also includes murals and borders, which can transform any room.

Use a hard, durable, oil-based varnish for decoupage on floors. About 4 coats would give good protection. For walls, 2 coats of water-based varnish will suffice.

ABOVE *A new superwood blank toy box was bought for this project. But look in your store room – you may have an old wooden chest which could be put to good use. Remember to clean and sand it thoroughly before beginning to paint. Wallies were ideal for this toy box and can be used to repeat the theme on cupboards or other items in the room.*

BELOW *The cut-outs of roses worked well with the elegant lines of this scalloped galvanized tin, creating a soft, feminine look.*

Tools and equipment

Some special tools and equipment are required to make sure that your decoupage project is a success. You will find that most craft and hardware shops will stock these items.

Cutting knife

You need a special knife for the intricate cutting of detailed pictures. The best kind to use is a slim craft-knife – it looks like a scalpel – with replaceable blades. Cutting knives with snap-off blades are not suitable as they are not flexible enough. The blade needs to be changed as soon as it gets blunt or when the tip breaks off – otherwise you could rip your paper.

Scissors

A sharp, curved pair of cuticle scissors is ideal for cutting the rounded edges of your picture. Invest in the best pair that you can afford – they will remain sharp for years. Keep them just for decoupage and *don't* use them on your toe-nails!

Cutting mat

It is very important to invest in a self-repairing cutting mat – it will not blunt your blades like other surfaces will. A cutting mat 'heals' itself when you cut into it, so the surface remains smooth. Always keep your cutting mat free of paint and glue – a well looked-after mat will last for years. It is a little pricey but you will save a small fortune on blades and ensure a professional-looking end product.

Roller

We believe that it's essential to use a rubber roller to smooth out bubbles when gluing cut-outs. The rollers come in different sizes, but the 5 cm (2 in) rollers are the easiest to work with. It is possible to glue very small pictures without a roller but once you move to bigger cut-outs and completely covered items you can't do without one.

Glue

Transparent paper glue is ideal for sticking down smaller motifs – anything smaller than 20 cm (8 in). Choose slow-drying glue – this allows you time to reposition your picture if necessary. You will find this at stationery stores.

When decoupaging large cut-outs or covering items completely in paper, we find that wallpaper glue works best. Don't mix up the whole packet; a heaped teaspoonful of wallpaper paste mixed with water in the recommended ratio will usually do. Wallpaper glue is very slow drying and you need that time in order to smooth out bubbles or reposition the print.

Use white wood/paper glue when sticking down cork or felt on the bases of your completed items to give them a professional finish.

Sandpaper and steel wool

Fine-grade wet-and-dry sandpaper is required for smoothing surfaces, as well as for interim sanding. Apart from old wood, which needs coarse

LEFT A selection of tools and equipment you will need for decoupage: clockwise from the bottom left-hand corner: Prestik, paintbrush, artists' paintbrushes, metal ruler, cutting mat, gold and silver permanent markers, cutting knife, high-density foam applicators, wet-and-dry sandpaper, grade 00-00 steel wool, felt, sponge roller, rubber roller, cuticle scissors, nappy liners.

23

sandpaper to begin with, the projects in the book require 400-, 600- and 1 000-grit sandpaper. The coarse sandpaper that you will need for preparing old wood does not have to be the wet-and-dry variety.

You also need steel wool (grade 00-00) for polishing traditional decoupage. If you cannot find any, you can use 1 000-grit sandpaper instead. Do not use any other steel wool – it will scratch your work.

Wood filler/spackle

Use this to fill in any imperfections on the item to be decoupaged before you start. It may seem unnecessary at first but, believe us, no matter how many layers of varnish you use you will see all those little holes and cracks in the end. This is a water-based product so it dries very quickly and just needs a quick sanding for a perfect base.

Brushes and applicators

High-density foam applicators are used specifically for decoupage, as they do not leave brush marks. They come in a variety of sizes – we

BELOW *A sponge roller was used to paint this fire screen, giving a good texture to work on. Applicators were used only in the corners to make sure that the entire surface was evenly coated with paint.*

If you are redecorating an old fire screen, it must be sanded down thoroughly with imperfections filled in with wood filler before decorating could begin.

LEFT *Using a damp nappy liner over your paper when rolling down the print is particularly important when you work with large prints and sheets of paper in order to achieve a smooth finish. When gluing down large items such as the sheets of wrapping paper used here, wallpaper glue is recommended since it gives you more time to accurately position your paper (see page 89 for detailed instructions).*

use the 2,5 cm (1 in) and 5 cm (2 in) applicators most of the time. Don't throw away old or ruined applicators. The handle can still be used for tasks such as mixing and moving resin, for instance. It is advisable to use a normal paintbrush on very large projects such as furniture and floors. You could also use a sponge roller to apply paint to larger items. A sponge roller gives an attractive textured finish.

It is worth investing in good quality brushes. If you look after them they will last longer and they will make a marked difference to your end result. Fine artists' paintbrushes are invaluable when it comes to painting finicky details such as corners or borders.

There are various specialized paintbrushes available for specific paint techniques such as stippling or dragging, though they tend to be a little cumbersome on smaller decoupage items (see pages 37-43 for paint techniques).

Nappy liners

Yes, nappy liners! These are invaluable during the gluing process as they protect the print when you use the roller to glue cut-outs to a surface.

We also use them to lift delicate cut-outs and place them onto a surface, as well as for some paint techniques. They can be washed and used time and again.

Felt and cork

Once your decoupaged item is complete, to give it a really professional finish glue either cork or felt to the base. Use white wood/paper glue. Leave to dry and trim off any excess glue afterwards.

Miscellaneous items

The following items are not essential, but we recommend that you try to get most of them since they will make it easier to achieve a professional finish:

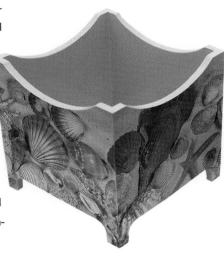

BELOW *If you are using complete covering (see page 57) use a damp nappy liner to wipe away off excess glue that has been squeezed out at the edges to avoid lumps of dried glue spoiling the neatly cut finish.*

*BELOW These striking Christmas tree dec-
orations were made with metal leaf (see
page 102 for detailed instructions).*

*If you like the gilded look but want
to take a short cut, there are special
papers available that have a metal-leaf type
finish, as used on these boxes, which were
completely covered with the paper. Make
sure that you seal the paper before
handling it – the gold rubs off easily.*

COLOURED PENCILS Soft, good quality
pencils are a lifesaver when it comes to
shading in those little mishaps which can
occur when you have sanded through a
picture or torn it in the gluing process.
It can also cover a white edge left during the cutting process. Don't use
water-soluble ones or kokis as they run
when you varnish over them.

METAL RULER A ruler is necessary for
cutting long straight lines and trimming
around the routed edges of a box. It
has to be metal because wooden and
plastic ones just end up with chunks
cut out of them by your blades.

PAPER TOWELS Kitchen rolls are very
useful for cleaning up and we also use
them regularly in our paint finishes.

HB PENCIL An HB pencil is used to
mark the position of your motifs
before you stick them down. It can also
be used for shading-in when a picture
has been torn or sanded away.

GOLD AND SILVER PERMANENT MARKERS
You can use these for signing your
work or drawing a border. Always
seal it after use with Modge Podge
before using any other varnish; otherwise the ink will run.

GOLD TAPE This is a self-adhesive tape
available from motor-spare shops. It
makes a very attractive border.

METAL LEAF (ALSO REFERRED TO AS GILDING)
Decoupage is often enhanced with
gold leaf, but true gold leaf is very
expensive and difficult to obtain.

You can achieve basically the same
look by using the cheaper alternative,
known as Dutch metal or metal leaf.
The metal leaf is sold in booklet form
with protective paper between the
leaves. When using metal leaf, you
will also need Wunder size (gold
size), which is the glue required for
adhesion of the metal leaf, as well as
shellac and white spirits for sealing
(see page 105 for easy gold-leafing).

Varnishes, resin and paints

There is a large selection of paints and varnishes available. In fact, just looking at what's on the shelves can make your head spin! We have therefore tried to make life easier for you by suggesting specific products. From there you can go on to experiment and discover what else works for you. Some products give wonderful finishes but are rather expensive so you might want to reserve them for those really special items. There are always cheaper alternatives, though, and we usually mention these as well.

Water-based varnishes

The product that we recommend is made by Heritage and is called Modge Podge. It is a must for all decoupeurs

ABOVE *A selection of varnishes, resin and paints used to complete the projects shown in this book. It took us years to use all of these, so don't rush out to buy them all at once.*

ABOVE *Sealing your motifs with Modge Podge is as important for sheets of paper used for complete covering, as for cut-outs. This strengthens the paper so that it won't tear and damage when you handle it to mark your cutting positions to ensure that the patterns flow. Try to keep the pattern aligned on the various sides and always match the top first on items with an angle, such as the bin (see page 58 for detailed instructions on complete covering).*

as it's used all the time, even if you are going to be finishing with an oil or acrylic varnish. Don't worry about its milky appearance when you apply it because it will dry clear. It is a very easy varnish to apply – quick drying and perfect for building up numerous layers – and may be sanded to a matt finish. We also use it to seal our paper before cutting; it hardens the paper, making it easier to cut and less likely to tear.

Plascon have a water-based product known as Water-Based Glaze Coat (Gloss and Matt), which is perfect for sealing paper murals or paint effects on walls. It's thin, easy to apply and will cover a large area, but it is not suitable when building up layers. Always clean your applicators and brushes after use with either water or soap and water.

Water-based
polyurethane hard varnish

Heritage make the above product which is very hard-wearing as well as being scuff, chemical and heat resistant, which is unique in a water-based varnish. Another distinct advantage is that it's non-yellowing. The varnish is available in matt or gloss. It is milky in appearance but will dry clear. But be sure to apply the varnish evenly as any 'blobs' will dry white. If this happens, gently scrape the white spots away with a knife and apply another coat. This is a really easy varnish to apply with a good end result. Clean your applicators and brushes after use with soapy water.

Antique crackle

This is a finish achieved with a two-part, water-based product made by Heritage – it produces large or fine eggshell cracks. If you don't remember anything else about this product, always remember this: *Crackle hates water!* Get it wet and the cracks will dissolve. It must be sealed with either Heritage Seal-skin or an oil-based varnish (*see Antique crackle, pages 60-63, for step-by-step instructions*).

Acrylic varnish

CV82 Glaze Coat (made by Plascon) is a clear, glossy and non-yellowing acrylic varnish. It's ideal if only a few layers of varnish are required but since it's relatively inexpensive we also use it to build up layers on larger items. Be careful of runs, though, as the varnish is quite thin.

Should you choose to build up layers with this product bear in mind that your drying-time is longer than it would be for the water-based products mentioned earlier, although not as long as it would be for an oil-based varnish. If you use a brush to apply the varnish it should be cleaned with turpentine. However, if you've used a sponge applicator put the turpentine to one side and rather use water and

a household cleaner, otherwise the sponge will be ruined.

Oil-based varnishes (polyurethane)

Oil-based varnishes are more durable and heat-resistant than water-based ones, but the drawback is that they have a yellowing effect on your work. This can be attractive if you are specifically looking for an aged effect. The colour change is not as noticeable on a darker background. Bear in mind that the more coats applied, the more yellow your item becomes and over a period of time it will become yellower still.

Once you've decided on an oil varnish try to buy the lightest one available. We use Plascon Woodcare Ultra Varnish, which is available in gloss and suede. It is also important to use a varnish that is not too thick as this makes application difficult. Shake the can and if it sounds like cream you are on the right track. It is possible to thin the varnish with turpentine if it is too thick to work with.

Oil-based varnishes take between 12 and 24 hours to dry. Follow the instructions on the tin and stick to them, especially regarding the drying time. Even if it feels dry on the surface, that does not necessarily mean that it is dry all the way through. Applying another coat over one that is not completely dry can result in some pretty strange reactions. Oil-based varnishes are used to seal Antique Crackle.

Always clean brushes with turpentine. Don't even try to use sponge applicators with these varnishes, as the turpentine will dissolve the sponges.

ABOVE *The wall-clock has been resined (see page 30) and the plates were covered with 6 coats of hard varnish. The prints on the plates were not buried, as the plates are hung up high.*

29

Seal-skin

This product, made by Heritage, is a transparent, high-gloss, quick-drying varnish. It can be used to seal antique crackle without changing the original colour. Clean your brushes with methylated spirits.

Resin

Pratley makes a high-gloss polymer coating, called Pratliglo, which can withstand a certain amount of heat (although we wouldn't recommend putting a pot directly from a stove onto it). We have put hot cups onto Pratliglo-covered trays before only to find that they had left indentations. However, an hour or so later, the resin had 'healed' itself.

Using resin requires a little practice because you have to mix together equal amounts of a two-part product and then you only have a limited amount of time in which to use the resin before it dries. It's also imperative that you work in a dust-free environment to get the best results, which are outstanding. You get an immediate high-gloss finish and your picture is buried in one pouring. Messes can be cleaned with acetone but please protect the surface you are working on because acetone dissolves all sorts of things (paint, polish, varnish, nail varnish and false nails!).

We do not use brushes or applicators with this product but save all our old applicator sticks and use them to manoeuvre the resin (see Resin, pages 68-71 for step-by-step instructions).

Polyurethane enamel

Plascon's Glatex 8 is a most useful two-component product, which needs to be mixed in a 3:1 ratio before use. It dries to a hard finish, which is very durable and non-yellowing. It is also both chemical and scuff resistant. It comes in a small colour range – make sure that you buy only the clear gloss or matt.

Be very careful to follow the manufacturer's instructions and work in a well ventilated, but not dusty, environment. We recommend this for an item that has been entirely covered with paper rather than burying cutouts. It is ideal if you are looking for a high-gloss finish. Seal the paper with at least 3 layers of Modge Podge before using the enamel to prevent the varnish from penetrating the paper. Working with it will require a little practice, though. Brushes need to be cleaned with thinners.

Paints

We used water-based paints for all the projects in our book because they are quick drying and easy to apply. A good rule to remember is that you can start with water-based products and follow with an oil-based one, but never the other way round. You will always need a tin of broken-white PVA – it goes by different names depending on the brand used. We recommend Plascon's VIP Acrylic PVA because it is easy to sand and is used for all base coats (except on steel: see Decoupage on galvanized steel, page 80). When attempting larger projects it is best to buy a litre-

BELOW The chocolate box was sealed on the outside with oil-based varnish because any other varnish will dissolve Crackle. To avoid yellowing, hard varnish was used on the inside of the box, as well as on the smaller box where we did not use Antique Crackle.

tin of the colour you desire. Plascon have a great selection of colours in their Polvin range. You can have virtually any colour you want mixed for you, and the paint covers well. Don't worry about the fact that some of these paints have acrylic in them – they are still water-based.

Most people prefer to work on smaller items when they are beginners or when making gifts and this is where Heritage Craft Colour come in very handy. These small pots of paint come in 56 colours, including metallic and fluorescent colours. They are perfect for smaller items because you don't end up with several tins of leftover paint. They give you the freedom to experiment without spending a fortune. We use foam applicators for applying paint, except for large projects where a paintbrush is better. Both can be cleaned with soap and water.

ABOVE *Resin was used on the lid top of the bread bin for a hard, durable finish to make it suitable for frequent use. The sides were sealed with hard varnish.*

Hanging your work

For most of your projects you will be applying numerous coats of paint and varnish and it is imperative that you allow sufficient drying time between coats. In order to prevent the item that you are working on from sticking to a surface, we recommend 'hanging' your work – resting it on top of a paint tin. This will allow a good circulation of air for drying.

Preparation

In decoupage the old adage 'practice makes perfect' might as well read 'preparation makes perfect'. Preparation is crucial to make sure that your finished product will last and look every bit as attractive as you had intended it to look. In addition to the actual preparation of the base on which you are going to work, preparation should also include practising cutting techniques, trying your hand at

arranging your cut-out motifs, making sure you become adept at gluing your cut-outs without ending up with half of them stuck where you don't want them, and becoming a good all-rounder with paint techniques. But don't despair – it sounds a lot harder than it really is and we can assure you that you'll reap the rewards if you don't just rush into your first project.

Preparation also means that you have to think through your project beforehand and try to visualise the end-product. Once you've chosen an item to be decoupaged, and selected the prints to be used, you will have to decide on the basic colour scheme you will use. These will determine which paint technique you can use, if any, or what kind of overall finish could be achieved. You should be mindful of which products (base coats, top coats, varnishes and so on) can be used together, and use them in the right order.

Preparing base materials

This is definitely not the most exciting part of decoupage but don't take short cuts with your preparation, as your end result depends on it. In this section we concentrate on new wood or superwood, since this is used for most of the decoupage finishes discussed in further chapters. When working with base materials other than new wood, prepare the surface according to the specific instructions given for that particular project or decoupage finish. When working on old wood, prepare the surface as described on page 99, then follow the steps discussed below. Be fussy about your work, paint evenly and neatly, avoiding any runs.

You will need
broken-white acrylic PVA
foam applicators
wood filler
400-grit sandpaper
acrylic PVA in colour of choice
Modge Podge

1 Unscrew and remove any hinges on the item to be decoupaged. (These are to be put back only once you have finished the project.) Apply a base coat of broken-white PVA to the entire surface of the item (inside and out, including the base). Leave to dry.

2 Fill all holes, blemishes and recessed nails with wood filler. This is important as the quality of the final finish depends on it.

3 When dry, dry-sand with 400-grit sandpaper until smooth. Sand the entire item, not only where you've used wood filler. Make sure that routed edges are well sanded.

4 Paint your item with the desired colour (inside and out). Three to 4 coats should cover it properly. If you are using a special paint finish, apply this now.

5 Apply a coat of Heritage Modge Podge over the entire item (base, inside and out) to protect your painted surface.

ABOVE *We did say that you could decoupage just about anything and this is a good example of an unusual decoupage blank which produced a really striking end-* *product. To turn this old vinyl record into a wall clock for a boy's room it was sanded first (with 300-grit sandpaper) to key it for paint adhesion, and then decoupaged as* *normal. When purchasing a clock mechanism (available from most craft shops and hardware stores) be sure to buy one that has a notch at the back for hanging.*

Paint techniques

In this section we discuss the more popular and easier paint finishes that are suitable for decoupage. We found that books on paint techniques can be very confusing and technical, so we've tried to keep it as simple as possible.

There are no hard and fast rules when it comes to paint techniques, as it is a matter of personal taste. All the paint finishes demonstrated below are water-based.

Because water-based paints dry ex-tremely quickly, acrylic scumble glaze is used to prolong drying time and to keep the paint 'open', allowing you time to manoeuvre it. It is very difficult to give exact ratios of paint, scumble glaze and water since these differ depending on the colour intensity desired and the size of the surface area to be covered: the larger the area the more scumble glaze you'll need in order to keep the glaze 'workable'. If you ask the experts they will invariably tell you they go by 'feel' rather than measurements. However, if you are just beginning and need definite instructions, the basic mix is roughly 1 part paint, 2 parts scumble glaze and 3 parts water.

It is very important that the surface over which you will do your paint finish has a solid coverage of the base colorant – remember that your finish should complement the picture, not overpower it. The keyword here is always 'subtle'.

LEFT The natural wood-finish on the magazine stand was achieved by dragging. We used various shades of brown, with a little rust, waiting for each coat to dry before applying and dragging the next coat.

BELOW A bird's eye-view of various paint techniques, from left to right colour wash, rubbing, bagging, dragging and antiquing.

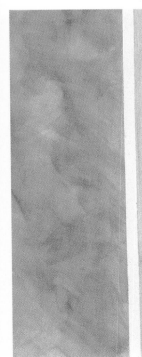

You will need

For all paint techniques:

tube of artists' acrylic paint

Plascon acrylic scumble glaze

water

paintbrushes (one small and one
    medium sized)

nappy liners or paper towels

black refuse bag

Modge Podge

Preparation

- Prepare the base material as described on page 36, up to and including step 3 (*see* page 83 for instructions on preparation of galvanized steel).
- Apply 3 to 4 coats of the desired base colour. Leave to dry, always allowing sufficient drying time between coats.

Colour washing

True colour washing is done by building up complementary colour washes over a solid, neutral base-coat, allowing time in between applications for drying.

For your mix, you need to increase the ratio of water to 5 – 8 parts water, and omit the scumble glaze completely. Apply the wash with a small brush, working quickly in all directions. As the

paint dries, brush it out in all directions with a dry brush (medium size) to smooth out the edges. Leave to dry.

Once the paint is dry, repeat the above process, brushing paint on the areas that were previously missed. Building up gradually, continue until you have the colour intensity you want.

A good way to soften the whole effect is to finish off by applying a thin cream-coloured wash to the entire surface, then dry-brushing it to remove any runs. Leave to dry and seal with a coat of Modge Podge.

BELOW *This planter was first colour washed with yellow ochre over a calico base coat, and then antiqued over the Wallie, a combination which gave a really attractive finish.*

Rubbing

This is an easier way to apply a wash. For your mix, use 1 part paint, 5 – 8 parts water, and include 2 parts scumble glaze.

Apply a coat of the mixture evenly to the prepared surface, then use a nappy liner and gently rub the glaze as if you are polishing.

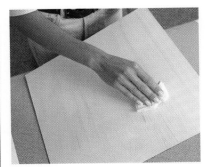

You can also simply rub on the paint with a dry nappy liner instead of first brushing it on and then wiping it off. Leave to dry and seal with a coat of Modge Podge.

ABOVE *The paint effect on this toy box was created by dabbing on a broken-white glaze over Lemon Ice. The edges were painted with a darker ochre colour with the broken-white glaze rubbed over to soften the effect.*

Bagging

Bagging gives a finely textured finish. Use 1 part paint, 2 parts scumble glaze and 3 parts water for this finish.

Once you have applied the paint, virtually anything can be used to create an effect. Here we used a black refuse bag, but anything from crumpled cling wrap to a crumpled nappy liner or soft cloth can be used.

Paint the mixture onto the surface and, using a crumpled piece of a black refuse bag, dab at the paint, changing direction with each dab, until you have worked the entire surface. You can also dab with a crumpled nappy liner or a piece of cling wrap for a softer effect. This is bagging off.

To bag on, the mixture is not painted onto the surface, but dabbed on. Dip the bag into the paint and press onto a piece of paper first to remove excess paint, then dab onto the surface, once again changing direction as you dab. Leave to dry and seal with a coat of Modge Podge.

Dragging

Use 1 part paint, 2 parts scumble glaze and 3 parts water for your mixture.

Paint the mixture onto the surface with a small brush. Firmly drag a dry, flat brush (normal medium sized brush, not necessarily a dragging brush) through the wet paint. Start at one end and continue in one motion to the other end, keeping a steady hand.

Repeat the dragging motion until the entire surface has been done. Repeat the dragging again if thick, dark lines remain in places, or if you want a more regular finish.

Leave to dry and seal with a coat of Modge Podge.

OPPOSITE PAGE *We used blue as a base colour and bagged on white paint, using a nappy liner for a subtle effect, which works well with the pictures. The inside lid has also been decoupaged, making for an attractive display if the box is left open.*

BELOW *The motif of a 'reading lady', glued onto a natural wood-finish achieved by dragging, seemed particularly appropriate for this magazine stand.*

RIGHT *The galvanized steel containers were all painted in neutral tones. Once the pictures were glued, we antiqued over the entire surface of each item to soften the overall effect.*

Antiquing

This paint finish will result in an aged look. Antiquing is a very popular finish for decoupage, especially if you are using traditional pictures, such as flowers, particularly old roses, fruit and cherubs. You can also apply the finish over your pasted pictures. This will give both the background and the motif an 'old' look.

The general mix for antiquing is I part raw umber artists' acrylic paint, 2 parts scumble glaze and 3 parts water. Traditionally, this finish is applied over a neutral tone such as broken white, but it can also look attractive over dark colours.

Apply the mixture with a brush, ensuring that the whole surface that you are working on is covered. Leave for about I minute and before it begins to dry, rub off with a nappy liner or a piece of kitchen towel. Rub in both directions in a polishing motion. To ensure a smooth finish, fold the nappy liner rather than crumpling it.

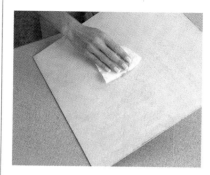

For an authentic look, leave some paint that may have collected in the corners and in routed edges.

Sponging

When you mention the words 'paint techniques', the first thing most people visualise, is sponging. The secret to successful sponging is subtlety. If possible, always use a sea sponge.

Sponging is a particularly good paint finish to use on glass since it gives an attractive texture and good coverage. Applying paint with a brush or even a sponge applicator may leave unattractive lines and markings.

Dip the flat base of the sponge into the paint and dab it on a piece of kitchen paper to remove excess paint. Lightly dab the sponge onto the surface you are sponging, changing direction with every dab to create an attractively varied pattern.

Leave to dry and, depending on the effect you wish to achieve, repeat the process with a contrasting colour or a colour in the same tone.

Tea-staining

This is not really a paint effect, but since it is also applied before the cutting and gluing process, we thought it best to include it here.

Tea staining is used to give black and white pictures an authentic aged look. Pour boiling water over a tea bag and allow to cool. Squeeze some of the water out of the bag and gently wipe over the picture. Do not rub vigorously, as this may damage the paper and spoil your motif.

Leave the motifs to dry completely before sealing with Modge Podge and cutting out.

ABOVE *The black and white motif on this plate was tea-stained.*

BELOW *This attractive paper clock-face was a perfect match for the black and white images, so we used it on a square, new wood decoupage blank. The images were tea-stained and then the clock was antiqued ever so slightly to give it an authentic aged look. Clock mechanisms are available from hardware and craft shops.*

Cutting techniques

As you know by now, decoupage is the art of decorating a surface with paper cut-outs to create the impression of hand painting. For this reason your cutting technique is very important.

Initially the cutting-out process may seem a rather daunting task, but once you have the hang of the technique, it can be highly enjoyable and extremely therapeutic. We have a friend who loves cutting so much that she has a wonderful selection of cut-outs but very few finished items!

Invest in a ringbinder with plastic inserts to store your cut-outs. You will often have extra motifs that can be used on later projects.

LEFT *The motif for this tray was a real challenge to cut out. We cut away the inside bits first before moving to the outside edges.*

BELOW *It was very tempting to cut around the branches of the palm trees rather than cutting them out individually. Spending a little more time on your cutting will make a big difference to the end result.*

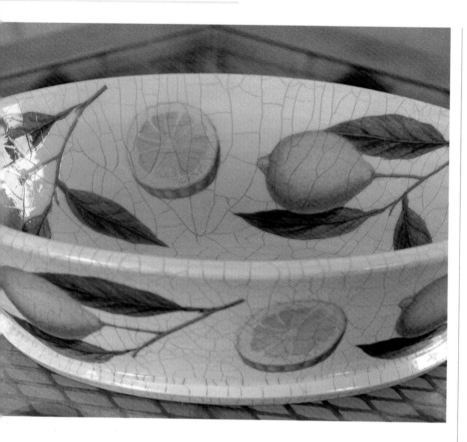

for cutting the rounded edges of fruit or a butterfly's wings.

Using scissors

First cut out the inside bits, using a cutting knife. The reason for this is that if you leave the inside bits for last you are likely to tear the outer edge of your motif. Once the inside bits are cut out, move to the outer edge, using scissors or a knife – whichever you are most comfortable with.

Seal your paper on the printed side with a coat of Heritage Modge Podge before you start cutting. This is done to strengthen your paper and protect it when gluing. Don't worry about the milky appearance of the Modge Podge – it dries clear.

The paper must be dry before you start cutting out the picture. First cut the motifs you want to work with into a manageable size. Don't try to cut out a tiny butterfly from a full sheet of wrapping paper. Always cut out the inside bits first – this makes it easier to handle the cut-out.

Using a cutting knife

Cut firmly when you use a cutting knife. Applying too little pressure will result in damaged or torn paper. Cut either on or inside the edge of the picture to avoid leaving any background bits on the cut-out.

Don't worry if you have a slip of the blade and cut off a part of the picture – it's not the end of the world since you can glue it together again later.

A cutting knife is useful for sharp, intricate details such as stems or borders, while a pair of scissors is perfect

The hand that holds your scissors should be kept still and relaxed, only the fingers working the blades should move. You may find it easier to support your arm on a table.

Loosely hold the paper in the other hand, turning the paper rather than the scissors when you cut.

Handy hints

- When using tissue or thin wrapping paper, seal both sides with at least 2 to 3 coats of Modge Podge before cutting out to strengthen the paper.
- Should the image you want to use be too large for the item to be decoupaged, cut it down and resize it by leaving out parts of the design (leaves, stems and so on).
- Make sure that all corners are cut out properly before lifting your cut-out from the paper – it is very easy to tear the corners.
- When cutting intricate designs, leave thin sections of paper uncut (like bridges), between a stem and a leaf, for example, in order to prevent the intricate bits from tearing off. Once the bulk of your motif has been cut out, simply cut the 'bridges' away before gluing.
- If you overlap pictures when gluing them down, you need double the normal amount of varnish to bury them. Rather cut away what you would have overlapped.
- Use a self-healing mat to prevent blades from getting blunt too quickly.

OPPOSITE PAGE *The design of the lemons was too big to fit on the outside of the bowl. This problem was easily solved by removing one leaf from the picture. This is a good example of 'cutting down' an image.*

BELOW *An example of how intricate and basic cutting can compliment each other. The image on the tray took about an hour and a half to cut out whilst the cutlery canteen took five seconds! Resin was poured into the base of the tray so that it can be used to hold hot garlic bread.*

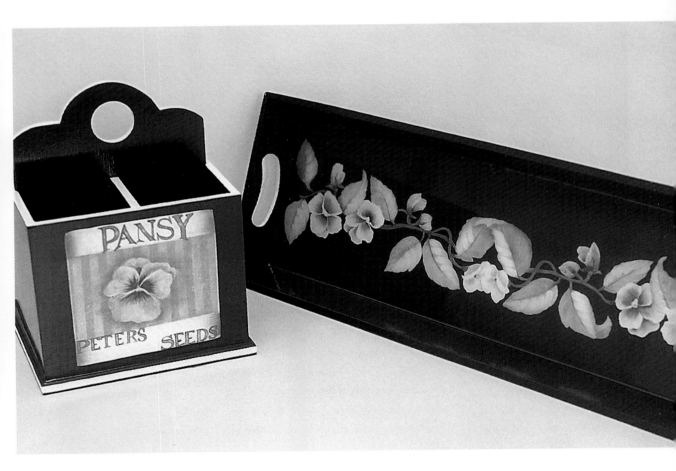

Arranging and gluing

ABOVE When arranging on ostrich eggs, either use one picture as a focal point or place the motifs randomly over the entire egg so that any side can be displayed.

Now it is time to start thinking creatively. All your hard work during the various stages of preparation will be married together in your design. Before arranging your design, make sure that you have a lot of pictures already cut out. This gives you the freedom to experiment with your design.

If you wish to overlap instead of cutting away, first place the pictures that go underneath.

Arranging

Occasionally your design will come together immediately, but this is the exception rather than the rule. Sometimes it will seem as if nothing is going to work. Don't despair – leave the arranged pictures, have a cup of tea, and come back later to try again.

On vertical sides you will need to use Prestik to hold your motifs in place so that you can see the overall result before you begin gluing. A design doesn't necessarily have to be absolutely symmetrical – something placed just off-centre can be very attractive. A good way of filling in a gap is to add a small motif – this can also soften the overall design. Be careful of 'over-decorating' – most beginners tend to do this because they are so enthusiastic. Remember the saying, 'less is more'.

Gluing

Once you are happy with your arrangement you can begin to glue. Before completely removing your motifs, lightly mark their position in pencil on the item you are decorating so that you know exactly where to place them once you've applied the glue. If you damage any of your cut-outs slightly when gluing, allow it to dry first and then touch up with your coloured pencils.

1 Lay your motifs, picture-side down, onto a damp nappy liner. This prevents the picture from getting stuck to the surface you are working on. It is easier to glue smaller cut-outs first. The best way to apply the glue to the picture is by using your fingers. Apply the glue liberally onto the entire back surface of the picture.

2 Place the picture lightly in the desired position. Cover the picture with a new damp nappy liner to protect it. Glue the picture down using your roller, making sure that all wrinkles and air bubbles are smoothed out. A good tip when gluing is to start rolling from the centre outward. Never stick down the sides first

as air will get trapped in the middle and you will end up with excess glue on your surface.

3 Using a mild vinegar solution (a teaspoon of vinegar to a cup of water), wipe off any excess glue. Ensure that every edge is firmly glued down. Leave to dry and seal with a coat of Modge Podge.

Handy hints

- To avoid creases and folds, use your fingers and a damp nappy liner rather than the rubber roller to glue pictures to any curved objects.
- To ensure that an image running over both the lid and the base of a lidded item is a perfect fit, glue the image in one piece and cut it open afterwards (see page 59).
- After applying glue to an intricate cut-out, don't lift it off the nappy liner to place it; rather lift the whole nappy liner with the cut-out and press it into position.

Decoupage finishes

We follow an approach in this book that differs from that of other decoupage books. Experience has taught us that beginners who blindly follow the instructions for specific projects often don't understand the principles behind the various finishes and don't realize that they can use the same finish on so many different blanks. For this reason we dedicated the bulk of the book to the different decoupage finishes.

To turn out professional, beautiful work you should first try your hand at traditional decoupage which will give you a good understanding of what the craft is about. Once you become more confident, use your imagination and combine different finishes. For example, you could use a cracked-paint-effect on the sides of a box and completely cover the lid. Or pour resin over the lid of a box finished with Antique Crackle, and seal the sides with oil-based varnish or Seal-skin. Using Antique Crackle over pictures will help to bury prints. You can bury them completely by applying several coats of oil-based varnish over the crackle, but don't forget that every coat makes your work more yellow, and, with time, these varnishes go yellower still. Routed edges look good painted in a contrasting colour. Gold is the most popular, but use your imagination, experiment with various contrasting colours and don't get stuck in the gold-only rut.

Traditional decoupage under varnish

This original form of decoupage is centuries old. Earlier, only oil-based varnishes were available making any decoupage project extremely time consuming, since these varnishes take at least 12 hours to dry. Fortunately water-based varnishes available today dry quickly, making it a lot easier and less time-consuming to create this traditional look. The aim of this form of decoupage is to bury or float the picture, making it look as if it has been hand-painted. The finished product has a subtle sheen to it – it looks like a French polish.

This technique gives a more classic finish than the finish achieved with modern high-gloss products. Everyone should make at least one item using the traditional method – you can't call yourself a decoupeur until you have. Once you have mastered this technique and achieved its subtle sheen, you may find that commercially sold decoupage with only a few layers of varnish looks unfinished.

BELOW *The pictures for this umbrella stand came from an old calendar. We buried the prints with 40 layers of acrylic varnish and six years later the umbrella stand is still in an excellent condition.*

RIGHT *The box with its elegantly rounded lid was crying out for classic decoupage because of its interesting lines. To ensure a perfectly matching continuous image, the little cherub on the side, as well as the basket of fruit were stuck down in one piece over the base and the lid, then cut open once the glue had dried.*

Dragging resulted in a natural wood-finish on the magazine stand, which was then completed the traditional way over a classic decoupage image.

Bisque-fired ceramic lamp bases as well as lampshades are available from hardware stores and craft shops. The classic shape of this lamp base made it ideal for a traditional finish. The lamp base is very fragile at the top, so be careful when you wire it (wiring for lamp bases can be bought at a lighting shop or hardware store). A matching base and shade could be very attractive.

You will need

decoupage blank, paper/prints
foam applicator
Modge Podge
400- and 600-grit wet-and-dry
　　sandpaper
1 000-grit sandpaper or grade
　　00-00 steel wool
plain white toothpaste

soft cloth
cork or felt
white wood/paper glue

Preparation

- Prepare the decoupage blank as described on page 34.
- Prepare and glue motifs as described on pages 46-49.

1 Using a foam applicator, apply 20 coats of Modge Podge to the entire decorated surface of the item. Work in alternate directions (one coat top to bottom, followed by one coat side to side) allowing each coat to dry. The reason for applying the Modge Podge in alternate directions is to get complete coverage.

2 Dip the 600-grit sandpaper into cool tap water and wet-sand the item where you have applied the 20 coats of Modge Podge. Sand firmly but carefully backwards and forwards, not in a circular motion. Keep the sandpaper moist at all times to avoid scratching your work. The Podge will turn milky in appearance, but will dry clear. Continue sanding until the

object feels smooth to the touch and you cannot see too many shiny marks. Take care that you don't sand through to the picture, and go easy on the edges. Rinse, wipe off excess water and leave to dry.

3 Apply 10 coats of Modge Podge as before. Repeat wet-sanding with 600-grit sandpaper as in step 2. Rinse, wipe off water and leave for about 12 hours. Apply another 10 coats of Modge Podge.

4 Once you are satisfied that you have a sufficient build-up of varnish to bury your print, wet-sand with 400-grit and then 600-grit sandpaper until your work is absolutely

matt and there are no tiny 'shiny' spots whatsoever. Hold your work up to the light to make sure that you have not missed any spots. Rinse, wipe off water and leave to dry for 24 hours.

5 Dry-polish your item with 00-00 grade steel wool. Do not use any other type – it will leave scratch marks. If you are unable to obtain this steel wool – wet-sand the item again with 1 000-grit sandpaper, rinse, wipe and leave to dry for 12 hours.

6 Polish your finished item with a dab of toothpaste and a soft cloth. The more you polish your work, the greater the sheen will be. Cut a piece of cork or felt to fit the base of your item, using the base as a template. Glue to the item with white wood/paper glue.

Handy hints

- Be careful of trapping hairs in your work. Wash your applicator and squeeze it dry before use, you can get rid of hairs that may be stuck on the applicator. Any remaining hairs should be picked out carefully.
- Even if you are going to stick cork or felt underneath your item, it is imperative that you seal the base with at least one coat of Modge Podge because it will get wet during the sanding process.
- When you are applying the layers of Modge Podge, make a list of numbers on a sheet of paper, tick off the number of each coat you have applied, and write down in which direction you have applied it.
- Apply your Modge Podge as smoothly as possible – roughly applied Podge will require more sanding.
- If you apply a few coats of Modge Podge per day, put your applicator in a plastic bag after use and only wash it at the end of the day.
- Don't be tempted to apply a layer of acrylic or oil-based varnish over the coats of Modge Podge, as it will crack with time.

Complete covering

Some papers lend themselves to using the entire sheet because of the nature of the design. The whole design will be used instead of only part of the design. This is also a quicker way of completing an item – because there is no burying involved you need fewer coats of varnish.

When you make a matching set of decoupage – more than one item with the same paper – it is very attractive to use a cut-out on one item and complete covering on the other. This is a good option if you need to make a gift in a hurry.

For the method we are demonstrating, choose paper that does not obviously face one way or the other; otherwise it will be noticeable that the design is facing upside down on some of the covered surfaces. We chose a lidded box to demonstrate how you can make sure that the design on the lid and the base of the box remains a perfect match (see step-by-step instructions on pages 58-59).

Because you need a flat surface and good adhesion, the best base material to use for complete covering is new wood or superwood.

LEFT *The straight lines of this wine box made it easy to match up the images on all sides. When completely covering something with high sides like this, match up and glue the sides first, rather than trying to match the top with all the sides.*

BELOW *A good example of different styles complimenting each other. The bin has been completely covered while a single image from the same wrapping paper has been cut out and used on the tissue box, finished with resin. The gold tape (see page 26) that was used on the edges creates further continuity of design.*

You will need

decoupage blank

acrylic PVA in colour of choice

Modge Podge

Prestik

wrapping paper

cutting knife and mat

HB pencil

transparent paper glue or
   wallpaper glue

rubber roller

nappy liners

600-grit sandpaper

Preparation

- Prepare the base material as described on page 34, up to and including step 3.
- Paint only the inside of your item with the colour of your choice, leaving the outside with only the sanded base coat.
- Seal the inside of the item with Modge Podge.
- Now seal the outside, including the base, with Modge Podge.
- Apply a coat of Modge Podge to the printed side of your wrapping paper. This strengthens the paper before you start cutting.

1 Use the box as a template. Secure the lid to the base with a little bit of Prestik on each corner and press down firmly so that there is no opening. Place the box underneath the paper to be used. Lightly wrap the paper around the box to ensure that you have enough to cover all sides. Using your fingers, press the paper down over the top edges of the box, thereby marking the paper where it should be cut.

2 Turn the paper over with the printed side down. Place the box, top down, exactly where you have made the markings. Using the box as a template, cut carefully around the lid and remove the cut-out. Lightly pencil the word 'top' on the inside of the cut-out.

3 Place the box (top down) back into the cut-out space. Now turn the box onto its side towards you. Cut around this edge and return the box to the centre. Lightly pencil on the inside of the cut-out to which side of the box it corresponds

with. Using this method, work in a clockwise direction until paper coverings have been cut out for all the sides.

4 Apply the paper glue generously to the top of the box (not to the paper). Place the corresponding piece of paper lightly on top of the glue. Cover with a damp nappy liner and roll from the middle outwards with a rubber roller. Check your work as you go along to ensure that you are not rolling in any folds. Clean off excess glue that has been squeezed out of the edges (use the damp nappy liner). Leave to dry. The paper will have stretched in the gluing process, so turn the box upside down and carefully trim off the excess paper with a cutting knife.

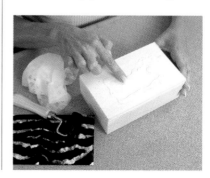

5 Ensure that the lid and base of the box are still joined together as you will be gluing the sides of the base and the lid as one. Line up the paper cut-outs so that the design matches the design on the top of the box. Glue two opposite sides straight after each other, using the roller as before. Find the gap between the lid and the base and make a slight indentation with your fingernail as a cutting guide when you open the box. Leave to dry and trim off excess paper. Repeat the process for the remaining sides.

6 Now you are ready to cut open the box. Using a cutting knife (with a very sharp blade) cut carefully along the indentations you have made between the lid and the base. Make sure that you cut right through the paper.

Carefully separate the lid from the base and remove the Prestik. You will now have a matching lid and base. Clean off any excess glue. Check that the paper edges have been firmly stuck down. Re-glue any bits that have lifted and leave to dry.

7 Apply 4 coats of varnish to all the decorated surfaces of the box, allowing sufficient drying time between coats. Very gently dry sand with 600-grit sandpaper. Apply another 2 coats of varnish to complete, again allowing sufficient drying time between coats.

When your item is completely dry, cover up any mistakes, such as slips with the cutting knife or sides not lining up with a gold or silver permanent marker prepared as described in the hints box below.

Handy hints

- When you are covering a large item (for instance a waste paper bin) wallpaper glue is recommended as it is slow drying, giving you more time to carefully position the paper and to reposition, if necessary.

- When covering a box with a routed edge, your lid and base don't necessarily have to match. It is a better idea to match the sides. Use a metal ruler to trim excess paper off the lid.

- If the sides aren't as neat as you would have liked, you can cover your mistakes with a gold or silver permanent marker. Cut a small slit down the centre of the marker's nib with a cutting knife and run the marker down the sides of your item. This will enable you to draw a straight line down two edges at a time.

Antique crackle

Creating an authentic crackled antique look involves the use of two separate products which react against each other, thereby creating the cracks. These cracks are then filled with paint to make them look authentic and aged. When people see the end result they will think you're a creative genius, but all it really takes is a little care and a lot of patience. Where we went wrong the first couple of times we tried this finish, was in not waiting long enough for the crackling process to end. It is very tempting, once the cracks start forming, to charge in with the oil paint and complete your project. Always remember, once you have sealed your item you can't go back and fill in new cracks. This finish can be applied to virtually any base material.

Cracks filled in natural earth tones (raw or burnt umber) will give you an authentic aged look while gold and copper looks very effective on a dark background.

RIGHT *Ceramic bowls are always very rewarding to work on because of their pleasing shape and lines. Since this bowl has images on the outside as well, the beauty of the work is not lost when the bowl is filled with fruit.*

LEFT *A decoupaged ceramic bowl such as this can only be used for fruit or other 'dry' food items, since it cannot be submerged in hot, soapy water to be cleaned. Simply wipe it clean with a wet cloth.*

You will need

patience

decoupage blank, paper/prints

Modge Podge

Antique Crackle base coat (choose
    large or small cracks)

Antique Crackle top coat

turpentine and nappy liners

artists' oil paint or Heritage Magic
    Touch (gold)

oil-based varnish or Seal-skin

Preparation

- Prepare the base material as
  described on pages 34-43.
- Seal, cut, arrange and glue your
  motifs as described on pages
  46-49. If necessary, 'cut down'
  the motifs to fit your item as
  described on page 47.
- Seal the entire item, including
  the base, with one coat of
  Modge Podge.

1 On your prepared base material, apply one coat of Antique Crackle base coat to the entire area to be crackled, working from top to bottom. Allow to dry and apply a second coat working from edge to edge. Allow to dry. Once the item is dry, try to keep your fingers off the surface you are working on. Oily finger marks can cause the Crackle to pull.

2 Apply one coat of Crackle top coat over the base coat, working from one edge right to the other. Hold your work to the light to ensure that you have covered the entire surface. Leave the Crackle to dry naturally for at least one full week. This is imperative since new cracks will appear every day. If further cracks appear after you've sealed the item, you cannot go back and fill them in

3 Use a nappy liner slightly dampened with turpentine to rub artist's oil paint or Magic Touch into the cracks. Use the paint sparingly – a little goes a long way. You will need to work fairly quickly.

4 Remove any excess paint with a nappy liner slightly dampened with turpentine. Use a brisk polishing motion. Allow about 72 hours to dry.

5 Seal the crackled surface with an oil-based varnish or Seal-skin. You will need at least 3 coats of varnish for good protection. Should you choose to use more coats of varnish, bear in mind the yellowing effect this will have. Allow sufficient drying time between coats.

Handy hints

- Never use water or water-based products over Crackle – it will dissolve.
- Never dry your Crackle artificially or in direct sunlight. Temperature affects the size of your cracks – crackle on a hot day and your cracks will be smaller than when you crackle on a cold day.
- When crackling a box, crackle only one side at a time to avoid runs.
- If you have a crackling disaster, don't despair. As long as you haven't yet filled in the cracks you can either remove the Crackle with warm water and start again, or re-apply the top-coat.
- Some people like to use gold dust to fill in the cracks. We prefer not to, because you cannot achieve such a crisp finish and, with time, it sometimes turns green.

ABOVE *Decoupaging a matching container for placemats is both functional and decorative. It not only keeps the set together but can be permanently displayed on a sideboard or diningroom table.*

Cracked-paint effect

This technique is not to be confused with Antique Crackle. In this instance the cracked look is achieved between two layers of paint rather than over a painted surface, giving you an attractive base to work on. Your item is decoupaged afterwards.

As this paint technique creates a very busy background, be careful not to over decorate. The rule of 'less is more' is very appropriate here.

Many people think that this paint effect is difficult to achieve, but if you follow our simple instructions you will be surprised at how easy it is.

We chose a nautical theme as the paint effect brings to mind weathered boats. We also combined cracked areas with areas left uncracked to heighten the cracked-paint effect.

A cracked-paint effect can be done on old or new wood, as well as ceramics and galvanized steel.

LEFT *The pictures used with the paint effect have been kept very plain. These items show that the images are also striking if not pasted directly onto a surface finished with a paint effect.*

BELOW *Cracked paint needs to be sealed with an oil-based varnish, but we didn't want the white areas to discolour. To get around this we used two sealers: water-based polyurethane hard varnish on the solid white sections, then an oil-based one on the cracked areas.*

You will need

decoupage blank, paper/prints
foam applicator
acrylic paint in contrasting colours
Heritage Kwik Crack
nappy liners
transparent paper glue
oil-based varnish

Preparation

- Prepare the base material as described on page 34, up to and including step 3. You will use this as the base for your paint effect.
- Seal and cut out your motifs as described on pages 46-47.

1 Apply 2 to3 coats of acrylic base colour. This is the colour that will show through the cracks. Allow to dry between coats.

2 Using a foam applicator, apply a coat of Kwik Crack to the area that is to be cracked and leave it to set for about 1 hour. The Kwik Crack must be dry to the touch.

3 Apply a coat of acrylic paint in a contrasting colour. Work evenly in one motion from one side to the other without stopping. You cannot paint in the normal way, moving the applicator or brush backwards and forwards, as there should be no overlapping; overlapping can result in smudged cracks which will ruin the overall effect.

4 Leave to dry for at least 2 hours without touching it! You will notice cracks appearing almost immediately. Like Antique Crackle this product doesn't like water or water-based products, therefore your base is not sealed with Modge Podge.

5 When gluing your motifs, be very careful not to spill any glue onto the cracked areas, as glue will spoil the paint effect. Apply glue very sparingly to the back of the motif, cover with a *dry* nappy liner and roll down. Immediately wipe off any excess glue with a dry cloth. Until you have sealed the cracked paint, be extremely careful not to get any water or dampness onto the paint.

6 To complete, seal with 2 to 3 coats of Plascon Ultra Varnish or any other oil-based varnish. Always allow sufficient drying time between coats. If you are fixing any attachments, such as the clock mechanism used here, wait at least 24 hours after applying the last coat of oil-based varnish before doing so.

Handy hints

- No water or water-based varnish can be used over the Kwik Crack.
- The best effects are achieved by using contrasting colours, not similar tones. Gold applied as base coat under any dark colour is usually very striking.
- The top-coat of paint may be watered down slightly to make application easier.
- Paint the Kwik Crack in the opposite direction to that of the paint and you will get a completely different look.

BELOW *Combining cracked and solid areas can be most effective, as seen on this writing-paper box. In this instance the image was applied to the solid white area to enhance the paint effect on the blue areas. These motifs were produced by an artist friend of ours. They were photocopied before use.*

Resin

In the past, the only way to achieve a smooth, high-gloss finish was by applying many layers of varnish, followed by a lot of elbow grease.

Now, all you need is one coat of resin. We recommend Pratliglo, a high-gloss, self-levelling, pour-on polymer coating (make sure you buy the two-part pack consisting of two bottles: one clear liquid and one yellow liquid). Our nerves were shot the first time we used it because one has to work against the clock.

Whatever you do, don't take a telephone call halfway through the process! Properly cured, the finish is beautiful, looks almost like glass and, with practice, becomes easier to achieve. It's also a hard and durable finish, ideal for trays.

Your biggest enemy is dust or fluff, so ensure that you work in a dust-free environment (there shouldn't be any fluffy jerseys or cat hairs). One pack of Pratliglo should cover a surface of just under half a square metre. Resin can be poured onto any flat surface.

Before attempting a large project, we recommend that you practise on a few smaller ones.

RIGHT *The initial idea with this bread box was to have the print on a flat, green background, but the fruit bowl was very stark and the fruit disappeared into the background. We overcame this by doing a fairly heavy paint wash, using burnt umber (reddish tinge), over the green background and the cut-out. This worked well with the picture and softened the colour of the fruit bowl to blend with the rest of the picture.*

BELOW *Because this cutlery box was made for a fellow decoupeur we had to pull out all the stops and do things she would not. Hence the intricate cutting, metal-leafing and resin to create a really classy finish. The inside of the box was fully lined with felt.*

You will need

decoupage blank, paper/prints

Modge Podge

varnish

dustcover (cardboard box or
plastic container to protect your
item while drying)

2 unwaxed paper cups

I pack of Pratliglo

ice cream stick or handle of
old applicator

toothpick

paper towel

Preparation

- Prepare your chosen base material as described on page 34.
- Prepare and glue your motifs as described on pages 45-49. Apply 5 layers of Modge Podge over the area to be covered with resin, so the Pratliglo will not penetrate the motifs.
- Areas that are not going to be covered with resin need to be sealed with at least 3 coats of varnish suitable for your project.

3 Use an applicator handle or ice cream stick to spread the resin, taking it right to the edge of the item you are covering. If you work carefully, the resin will remain at the edge of the box and level itself.

1 Place your work on a level surface before beginning to mix the resin and make sure you have your dust cover ready. Protect the surface with newspaper. Pour the clear liquid into one of the paper cups. Then pour exactly the same amount of the yellow liquid into the other cup.

Now pour the yellow liquid into the cup containing the clear liquid, scraping out any liquid that remains in the bottom of the cup.

Don't do this the other way round as the clear liquid is so thick you won't get it all out of the paper cup. Using the applicator handle or ice cream stick, mix thoroughly for about

I minute, stirring vigorously. You now have resin. (Don't worry about the bubbles; you'll take care of them later.)

2 You have to work fast because the resin starts hardening after about 10-15 minutes. Pour the resin into the centre of the surface to be covered, then spiral towards the edges. Pour enough resin to coat the entire surface the first time in order to avoid having to re-pour after it has started to harden. But be careful not to pour too much; otherwise it will start running over the edges. With a little bit of practice you will get it right.

4 To release the bubbles, gently blow over the surface of the resin. Most of the bubbles will magically disappear, but the stubborn ones need to be gently pricked with a toothpick. Work fast, but be careful not to spoil the resin.

5 Check meticulously for any hairs, fluff, dust or other particles that might have settled on the resin while you removed the bubbles, and gently remove them with a clean toothpick.

When you are happy with your work, put the dustcover over the top, making sure that it doesn't touch the resin. Leave to dry for at least 2 days.

Whatever you do, don't fiddle with your work and don't remove the dustcover. You will only make dents and allow dust in, which will definitely spoil the finished product.

Handy hints

- High levels of humidity will cause an 'oil-slick' appearance. Try not to work with resin on a humid day.
- If you have a problem with the resin, such as hairs, bubbles, and so on, leave it to dry, sand it with 300-grit sandpaper, re-mix and re-pour.
- If your resin doesn't dry properly, you probably haven't used equal amounts of clear and yellow liquid. Wipe off with acetone, re-mix and re-pour.
- Any small runs that have dried can be cut off carefully using a cutting knife, and sanded down with 300-grit sandpaper.
- Even if your resin feels dry, remember that it needs time to 'cure'. Most items need 2 weeks curing time before you can safely use it.
- Pratley includes a comprehensive troubleshooting guide in each pack of Pratliglo. Read it thoroughly before starting your project.

ABOVE *These items will compliment any wine cellar and will make a wonderful gift. On the wrapping paper the grapes were joined together in a line. They did not fit the dimensions of the tray, so we separated and re-joined them, overlapping slightly, in order to fit the tray. The smaller box is an example of the same paper used differently – here the lid has been completely covered with the wrapping paper. Gold paint on the routed edges finishes off the projects attractively.*

Decoupage on ceramics

There is a large selection of bisque-fired, blank ceramics available on the market, usually sold for ceramic painting. These are also the ceramics that we use for decoupage. In most cities you will be able to purchase unfinished ceramics from potters, decoupage shops or craft shops. But if you live in a small town, like we do, you may have to find a potter who will make bisque-fired pottery for you.

Working on ceramics is usually very rewarding, but bear in mind that the items you produce are purely for decorative purposes. A bowl can be used for fruit or a jar for cookies, as these can merely be wiped clean. Decoupaged ceramics should not be submerged in water, as this will eventually destroy the varnish.

Owing to the shape of the unfinished ceramics (jars, bowls, plates and so on) you will most likely be working on a curved surface. We therefore suggest that you use the traditional form of decoupage (see pages 52-55) to complete your work, namely many layers of varnish to bury the paper motifs. Another attractive way to finish ceramics is by crackling them (see pages 60-63). This is quicker, as not so many layers of varnish are required to bury the cut-outs.

LEFT *A bought transfer was used to decorate an inexpensive clay flowerpot. The transfer was easy to apply and eliminated the need for any intricate cutting. The deep purple paint applied to the rim and inside the pot enhances the colour of the lavender and adds to the appeal of the overall finish.*

BELOW *The same technique was used with a different colour scheme and a different set of transfers. Sets of clay flower pots of different sizes, decorated in the same theme, make a great gift.*

You will need

bisque-fired blank ceramic,
paper/prints
foam applicators
broken-white acrylic PVA
400-grit sandpaper
acrylic paint in colour of choice
Modge Podge
transparent paper glue
nappy liners

Preparation

- Paint your ceramic item with a coat of broken-white acrylic. Leave to dry and sand with 400-grit sandpaper. Work carefully, bearing in mind that ceramic items are fragile.
- Seal and cut out the pictures as described on pages 46-47, or select ready-to-use transfers suitable for your project.

1 Paint the ceramic item with the colour of your choice. Two to 3 coats should give good coverage, but apply a third coat if any base coat is till showing. Leave to dry and apply one coat of Modge Podge to prepare the surface for your gluing.

2 Arrange your pictures, following the steps as described on page 49.

You will be gluing on a curved surface, which is slightly trickier than working on a flat one, so make absolutely sure where you want to place all the pictures before you start gluing.

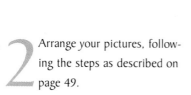

3 Glue down your motifs as described on page 49. You can use the roller on the flat surfaces of the item but not on the curved sides. Rather use your fingers and a damp nappy liner to press down the edges of your picture on the curved sides. This way you will avoid rolling in creases and possibly damaging your picture or breaking off pieces.

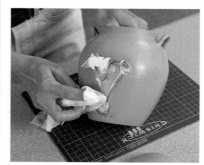

4 If you are using transfers rather than your own cut-outs, follow the instructions on page 18 to arrange the pictures and stick them down (no glue is necessary).

5 If you have chosen to use traditional decoupage under varnish, follow the necessary steps on pages 52-55. Should you wish to use an Antique Crackle finish, apply a coat of Modge Podge to the entire item, leave to dry and follow the steps on pages 60-63.

Handy hints

- When crackling on a curved surface don't apply the crackle top coat too thickly on the sides; otherwise it will run. It works best to apply the crackle from the centre, sweeping outward and up the sides.
- Remember to paint the underside of the ceramic for a professional finish. It is also necessary to seal the base if you are doing a wet sand (using traditional decoupage under varnish).
- Bisque ceramics are easily broken before being decoupaged – so handle them with care.
- If you are not bothered about burying your pictures, 6 coats of hard varnish will suffice.

BELOW *The delicate lines of the irises suited the canisters and plate perfectly. In order to use the same motifs on both canisters, we had to photocopy and reduce them for the smaller canister. All the items were finished off with 6 coats of hard varnish with a light dry-sanding between coats.*

Decoupage under glass

This form of decoupage is not seen as often as most other finishes, probably because it is more advanced, and should not be attempted by beginners.

The approach used in this technique is to follow the normal steps in reverse. Motifs are applied under the glass rather than on top, with the printed side showing through the glass. Then paint, either solid or in a paint finish, and varnish are applied.

We've found that a glass plate, or a shallow bowl with low sides, is more suitable than a deep bowl – you don't really want to see all the paint on the outside. Deeper items should be decoupaged on the inside. So if you want to decoupage a vase or a jar, bear in mind that you need to choose one with a wide opening in order to work on the inside.

You will not be able to put water in the vase, so it will only be suitable for dried flowers. Similarly, a jar can only be used to store dry food such as flour, pasta or rice. If you are making a bowl or a plate, it can be used for either fruit or as a cake plate.

Do not immerse these items in water. If you do, your paint will eventually peel off. Clean only the unpainted side by wiping it thoroughly with a wet cloth.

LEFT *Traditional kitchen images were used on these inexpensive glass storage jars. You could give them a completely different look by decorating them with jelly beans or other bright motifs. Sponge different paints in colours of the same tone on the inside to create a mottled background.*

You will need

glass plate (or item of your
     choice), paper/prints
foam applicators
Modge Podge
soluble marker
Prestik
nappy liners
metal leaf or metallic paint
acrylic paint
sea sponge
oil-based or hard varnish
turpentine

Preparation

- Wash the plate in soapy water to remove any grease; allow to dry.
- Seal your paper on both sides with Modge Podge, as both sides will get wet during the gluing process.
- Cut out the pictures to be used.

1 Divide the plate into 4 equal sections and mark the sections on the plate with a soluble marker. This will help you balance your design. Working on the right side of your plate, arrange the motifs on one quarter and repeat the design on the opposite quarter. Complete the arrangement on the two remaining quarters. Keep individual cut-outs in position with Prestik.

2 Trace the outline of the completed design with a soluble marker.

3 Removing one cut-out at a time, apply Modge Podge to the printed side of the picture (the Modge Podge is your glue). If your design is made up of overlapping cut-

outs, start with the cut-outs that went on top when you arranged the design, in other words what you arranged last must be pasted down first.

4 Turn over your plate. Gently press the motive in position on the wrong side of the plate, using the tracing to guide you. Cover with a damp nappy liner and roll firmly, using a rubber roller (this does not apply to a vase or jar where you can only use your fingers). Now turn the plate over with the right side facing you and ensure that no air bubbles are trapped underneath the cut-out. It may be necessary to press these out with your fingers. Wipe away any excess Modge Podge with a damp nappy liner. Allow to dry.

5 Ensure that all edges of your cut-outs are firmly stuck down to ensure that paint will not seep underneath the pictures. Remove all temporary markings with turpentine.

6 Apply gold-leaf to the edge of the plate (*see* page 105 for instructions on how to use gold

leaf), or paint with metallic paint. This is also done on the wrong side of the plate. If you are using gold leaf or metal leaf, don't seal this with shellac, since you will be covering it with numerous coats of paint.

7 Using several shades in the same tone (or the same colour if you prefer a flat background), lightly sponge on a coat of acrylic paint. Allow to dry. Repeat this process until you have complete coverage.

Seal with hard varnish or any oil-based varnish. We suggest that you apply 3 coats of varnish for adequate protection. Allow sufficient drying time between coats.

BELOW *The paper used for this glass plate looks good when used for complete cover, but once the individual images have been cut out, they are not easy to place. The motifs look better when overlapped rather than placed with spaces in-between. The plate was sponged with a mixture of broken white and raw umber. We started with a very light mix. Once this was dry, more raw umber was added to the mixture to make it darker for each further coat.*

Handy hints

■ It is important to remember that if you are overlapping cut-outs you need to glue in the reverse — anything that would normally be placed on top will be glued down first.

■ Should you wish to use a paint technique it is also done in reverse, in other words, apply the paint effect over the cut-outs, allow to dry and then apply 3 coats of broken white.

■ If you want to put fresh flowers in a decorated glass vase, place the flowers in water in a smaller vase and place this inside the decorated vase.

Galvanized steel

RIGHT *This tall multi-purpose container is a good example of the interesting, elegant shapes and lines available in galvanized steel. The indentations on the steel gave a good textured finish and compliment the antiquing. A glass bottle inside the container holds water for the fresh flowers.*

BELOW *The fairly large surface of the watering can lent itself to a special paint technique. We prepared a mixture of raw umber, yellow ochre, burnt umber and lots of scumble glaze for a dragging effect (no water was added). The mix was painted on, then dragged off with a dry brush.*

It has been our experience that many people find the thought of decoupaging on steel rather daunting. In fact, it's quite easy once you have correctly prepared the surface. Most of the steel items that are available have very interesting shapes and lines, which you would not often find on wooden products.

This is the one time that you don't have to worry about bumps and dents, as they add to the rustic appeal. Galvanized steel items are rel-atively inexpensive and are widely available from general traders, hard-ware stores, florist's and craft shops.

Please note that the step-by-step instructions deal with galvanized steel only and not other metal products. It is sometimes also referred to as galva-nized iron, but they are one and the same thing.

The extended caption on page 83 details steps to be taken when you work on enamel – also a very reward-ing surface to decoupage.

You will need

galvanized steel item

paper/prints

stiff bristle brush

Plascon Galvanized Iron Cleaner

paintbrushes (small and medium)

Plascon Galvogrip Metal Primer

Plascon Merit Universal Undercoat

acrylic paint in colour of choice

Modge Podge

varnish

mineral turpentine

transparent paper glue

Preparation

- Using a stiff bristle brush, thoroughly clean the galvanized steel with Plascon Galvanized Iron Cleaner as explained in the manufacturer's instructions. This is essential to remove the temporary protective coating.
- Seal and cut your pictures as described on page 46, or keep transfers ready if you're going to decorate your item with transfers.

1 Stir the Galvogrip Metal Primer thoroughly before use. Using a small paintbrush, apply a thick coat of primer to every surface of the galvanized steel (outside and inside, not forgetting the handle if there is one). Allow to dry for 24 hours. Thoroughly clean the brush with water immediately after use.

2 Stir the Merit Universal Undercoat well and apply a thick coat, again to all surfaces, inside and out, including the handle. Allow to dry overnight. Thoroughly clean the brush with mineral turpentine immediately after use. Do not skimp on the primer and the undercoat, as these preparatory steps will help to protect the paint on your finished item against chipping and peeling.

3 Paint the item in the colour of your choice, using a water-based paint. This is the only exception to the rule of never applying a water-based product over an oil-based one, since the universal undercoat allows you to do this.

Apply 3 to 4 coats of paint for good coverage, allowing sufficient drying time between coats. When the item is completely dry, apply a coat of Modge Podge to protect the paint and to prepare the surface for gluing on the motifs.

4 Arrange and glue down your pictures. Seal the pictures with a coat of Modge Podge and complete your project by using any of the following finishes:

- traditional decoupage under varnish (*see* page 52);
- apply 6 coats of oil-based varnish, allowing sufficient drying time between coats;
- Antique Crackle (*see* page 62);
- apply 6 coats of water-based polyurethane hard varnish, allowing sufficient drying time between coats.

Handy hints

- If your decoupage is to be displayed or used out-doors, you have to seal it with several layers of an oil-based varnish for extra protection (although we don't recommend leaving it out in the rain).
- Don't take any short cuts in your preparation; if you do, the paint will eventually peel off.
- Remember to prepare and seal the inside of your item as well.

BELOW *When you work on enamel, prepare the surface as follows:*

- *Dry sand with 100-grit sandpaper in order to 'key' the surface (inside and out) to ensure paint adhesion.*
- *Apply 1 coat of general-purpose steel primer (not Galvogrip) to the entire bowl, inside and out, and leave to dry for 24 hours.*
- *Apply 1 coat of Universal Undercoat, leave for 24 hours.*
- *Now continue as from step 3 for galvanized steel.*

Specific projects

In this chapter we will take you through step-by-step instructions for several specific projects which we've chosen for a variety of reasons. First, a concertina file, chosen for its transformation potential. Next come ostrich eggs, chosen for their wonderfully interesting texture and shape. Then we run through two larger items – a fire screen and a toy box – to deal with a slightly different approach to larger

items. When decoupaging larger items it is not cost effective to either bury the pictures or use the water-based varnishes. Although we have buried the design on larger items in the past, namely a table-top and umbrella stands, this is extremely time-consuming and the items can take a couple of months to cure. The items we've made will take a fair amount of wear-and-tear, especially the toy box, so a durable varnish is needed. We've only used six coats of varnish on each. You can use Plascon CV82 Glaze Coat instead of an oil-based varnish if you don't want a slight colour change, but bear in mind that oil varnishes are stronger and more durable.

Last but not least is Christmas – a theme section with ideas rather than ste-by-step projects. The suggestions and items included in this section will be equally successful when adapted and applied to themes such as Easter, Valentines Day, Mothers' or Fathers' Day, or special celebrations such as a silver or golden wedding anniversary.

Concertina file

Don't you just hate the way concertina files fall over once you have put a number of papers or documents in them, or tear after being handled a number of times?

By strengthening and decorating a plain cardboard concertina file with decoupaged hardboard sides you will end up with a file that not only does not fall over but looks good as well. And you will be able to use it year after year. A decoupaged concertina file also makes a most impressive and useful gift.

Use hardboard rectangles that will overlap the sides of the file by 2 cm (1 in) all round. The gluing process is a little hair-raising at first, but once you have mastered it you'll be amazed at how quickly you can turn a boring cardboard file into something really special. It is also a good way of using those odd sheets of wrapping paper that you've been storing in your cupboard for a while.

LEFT *This concertina file with its interesting array of musical instruments was made for a music teacher. If you can, choose paper appropriate to the job or hobby of the person you are making the file for.*

BELOW *These files make perfect gifts for men. Our husbands often ask us to make them for clients' personal documents. The ribbon can be replaced with leather strips if you find them too feminine!*

You will need

two hardboard rectangles
foam applicator
broken-white acrylic PVA
400-grit sandpaper
Modge Podge
sheet of wrapping paper
wallpaper glue
nappy liners
rubber roller
cardboard concertina file
150 cm (1½ yds) ribbon to
　match your paper
clear adhesive glue
Heritage Hard Varnish
white wood/paper glue

Preparation

- Using a foam applicator, apply one coat of broken-white base coat to the smooth sides of the hardboard rectangles.
- Sand the top and edges of the board with 400-grit sandpaper until they are smooth.
- Apply one coat of Modge Podge to the painted side of the board.
- Apply one coat of Modge Podge to entire sheet of wrapping paper to be used.

1 Open the flap of the concertina file, measure in 18 cm (7 in) from the end of the flap and cut off. Fold and glue the remaining section of the flap to the back of the file, using clear adhesive glue.

2 Cut the sheet of wrapping paper in half. Mix a small amount of wallpaper glue (a

tablespoonful of powder to the correct amount of water as specified on the packaging) and apply some of the glue to the entire smooth side of one board.

3 Place one piece of wrapping paper over the board, centring the paper so that the overlap is equal all round.

Place a damp nappy liner over the paper and begin gluing down by rolling from the top corner to the bottom corner and moving across the board until you reach the other side.

Roll firmly and check your work as you go along in order to avoid creases and folds.

4 Once the paper is glued in place, turn the board over carefully and wipe away any excess glue from around the edges. Diagonally cut off the corners of the overlapping paper at the corners of the board, about 6 mm (¼ in) from the board.

5 Apply glue to the rough side of the board only to where the overlapping paper will be glued down. Glue the long sides first, one at a time, pulling the paper firmly over the edges, like covering a book, and press down with your fingers, smoothing out any creases.

6 Now fold in the corners, fold over the short sides and glue down. Wipe away any excess glue and allow to dry. Don't leave the board on a flat surface as it may stick to it – balance it on top of a clean paint tin or similar object.

7 Once both boards have been covered, varnish only the parts of the boards that are covered in paper. Don't forget to varnish the edges to make them durable. You will need to apply about 6 coats, allowing sufficient drying time between coats. It is a good idea to do a light dry-sanding after 4 coats.

8 Cut the ribbon into 4 equal lengths. Measure on your file where the ribbon should be placed and lightly mark these positions on the top inside edge of both boards. Applying clear adhesive glue to one end of each length of ribbon, glue them in position, ensuring that the ribbons on the two boards are in exactly the same position. You will need to glue down about 7 cm (3 in) of the ribbon for a firm hold.

9 Apply white glue to one side of the file, position the glued side on the rough side of one of the boards with an equal amount of board overlapping all round and press down firmly. Take care not to get any glue onto the ribbons. The glue will take a few hours to dry and needs firm pres-

sure applied for good adhesion. Stack a pile of heavy books on top of it – be careful not to shift your board when doing this. Apply glue to the other side of the file and position the remaining board, rough side down, on the file, exactly matching the position of the board on the other side. Allow to dry as before.

Handy hints

- Cut the ends of the ribbon diagonally and burn them carefully to prevent them from fraying.
- If you are using paper with a direction specific design, be careful not to glue the boards onto the concertina file with the design upside down – it's easily done!
- Don't stack varnished boards on top of one another; if you do, they will stick.
- Don't use the file for at least two days after completion.
- If you have damaged the paper during gluing – remember your coloured pencils will cover a lot of mistakes. Remedy these before you apply the first coat of varnish.

Ostrich eggs

We have found ostrich eggs to be very popular as a gift for overseas tourists. The most popular pictures are of wild life ones, such as the Big Five.

Unfortunately, most people seem to be stuck in the wildlife theme and don't use their imagination – flowers and butterflies look just as striking on these eggs. And if you feel adventurous, you may want to try one with a Fabergé look!

You can use wrapping paper with gemstone and jewellery images which you can cut out and arrange in a rich, overlapping design.

Ostrich eggs come in various textures, shapes and sizes; we have found that the rounder the egg, the more difficult it is to work with.

Look for the more textured eggs, as they seem to be quicker to bury. Most African curio shops stock undecorated eggs.

OPPOSITE PAGE *The black and white images used for these understated ostrich eggs weren't stained because we wanted a stark contrast between the white eggs and the black images. This creates the impression that the pictures were painted rather than pasted onto the eggs. A non-yellowing acrylic varnish was used to keep the background crisp.*

RIGHT *A bright yellow background creates a completely different look. The dinosaurs are perfect motifs for eggs used to decorate a child's room.*

You will need

ostrich egg, paper/prints
400- and 600-grit wet-and-dry
   sandpaper
wooden dowel placed in
   sand-filled wine bottle
Prestik to secure egg to dowelling
acrylic paint in colour of choice
foam applicator
Modge Podge

nappy liners
transparent paper glue
Plascon CV82 Glaze Coat
I 000-grit sandpaper
toothpaste
soft cloth

Preparation

- Wash the egg thoroughly and leave
  to dry.

- If the egg is to be painted, dry-
  sand the entire surface lightly with
  400-grit sandpaper to key the surface for good paint adhesion.
- Put the dowelling into the wine
  bottle filled with sand and secure
  the egg onto the dowelling by
  using a small piece of Prestik
- Seal and cut your pictures as
  described on pages 46-47.

1 Paint the egg the desired colour – 3 coats will usually cover – and seal it with a coat of Modge Podge. If you have decided not to paint the egg and work on its natural colour, you must still give it a light sanding and seal it with Modge Podge.

2 Position the motifs in place with a little Prestik, lightly marking their positions with a soft pencil that will wipe off. Once you are satisfied with your design, begin gluing, following the steps on page 49.

3 Use a combination of the roller and your fingers to glue down the motifs, always working over a damp nappy liner. Leave to dry and touch up any mishaps with coloured pencils. Remove all pencilled position markings.

4 Apply one coat of Modge Podge. Apply 20 coats of CV82 Glaze Coat to bury the pictures, waiting at least half and hour in between coats. Work carefully to avoid runs. Wet sand using 600-grit sandpaper. Leave to dry. Apply another 10 coats and wet sand. Repeat until your pictures are buried, then wet sand with 400-grit sandpaper, followed by another sanding with 600-grit sandpaper. Leave to dry.

5 For a gloss finish apply two thin coats of CV82, allowing sufficient drying time between coats. If you prefer a matt finish, sand with I 000-grit sandpaper and polish with toothpaste and a soft cloth.

We used three different techniques on these eggs: antique crackle for the butter- flies, traditional decoupage for the shells and for the roses, antiquing over the entire egg and cut-out once it was stuck down. Both the antique crackle and the antique wash serve to soften and blend if you feel your item is too stark.

Handy hints

- The larger and rounder the completed design, the more difficult it is to stick down the motifs. Rather choose smaller motifs to start off with and move on to the more involved pictures covering a greater surface area once you've developed more confidence and expertise. Using smaller motifs also makes it easier to work on a curved surface.

- Custom-made stands for displaying eggs are available from some craft and curio shops. You can also use a thick wooden or brass bangle as a base, but you will still need a sand-filled wine bottle with wooden dowel to decoupage the egg.

- CV82 takes about 1 month to cure, so don't wrap your egg in bubble wrap and send it overseas immediately!

- You can build up layers with Modge Podge instead of CV82 to bury your pictures and then finish off with 1 000-grit sandpaper and a toothpaste polish. But don't be tempted to finish off with CV82 over many layers of Modge Podge; otherwise your finish will probably eventually crack.

- Duck and chicken eggs can also be decoupaged in much the same way. Blow out the inside first by carefully making a tiny hole on each end and blowing furiously. Thoroughly rise out with water otherwise the eggs will stink. The hole can be filled with a little bit of spackle. Work gently with these eggs because they are very fragile. Use a wooden skewer to handle the egg.

Fire screen

Often you will buy a sheet of wrapping paper because you fall in love with it but have absolutely no idea what you will use it on. This is exactly what happened here. The paper obviously had to go onto something big and the dimensions of this fire screen were ideal. This is a perfect example of re-shaping a picture because the leaves and branches were very wishy-washy without too many definite lines, so we made our own.

A blank superwood fire screen was purchased from a craft shop for this project, but it is also possible to use an old wooden one and redeco-rate it. It would need to be sanded down thoroughly before decorating could begin, though. Be sure to move the fire screen out of harm's way when you have a roaring fire.

RIGHT *The motif used on this fire screen had to be reshaped to suit the size of the screen. We reshaped the background around the angels to form leaves.*

OPPOSITE PAGE *We kept the tones of this fire screen fairly neutral as it suited the decor of the room it was originally made for. A modern fire screen can be made by using brighter motifs and contrast-ing colours on the surrounding borders.*

Toy box

When we were looking for pictures to decorate the toy box we stumbled across a product called 'Wallies' which we had never used before. Always ready to experiment with new products, we decided to try them and were pleasantly surprised.

There is a large variety of designs available and they are really easily applied, as they are made of pre-pasted, vinyl-coated wallpaper.

Wallies are a fast and fun way to decorate. They also have large wall murals following the same design, which allow you to decorate your child's entire room in a matching theme. These wall murals can be used on floors and cupboards as well.

A new superwood blank toy box was bought for this project. But look in your store room – you may have an old wooden chest which could be put to good use.

Remember to clean and sand an old chest thoroughly, and to fill in dents and blemishes with wood filler before beginning to paint.

OPPOSITE PAGE *We wanted the toy box to compliment the furnishings in this nursery. As the curtains are fairly busy we didn't want to over-decorate the box, so we used paste colours which matched the curtains but did not overpower them.*

LEFT *Using smaller motifs, such as the stars, in a set pattern, is a good way of balancing the design.*

You will need

toy box or old wooden chest
broken-white acrylic PVA
wood filler
400-grit sandpaper
small sponge roller
Plascon Super Acrylic Polvin:
    Lemon Ice
nappy liners
Plascon Super Acrylic Polvin:

white or broken white
tube of yellow ochre acrylic
    artists' paint
tube of raw umber acrylic
    artists' paint
Modge Podge
Wallies, or cut-outs prepared as
    described on pages 46-47.
Plascon Woodcare Ultra Varnish
    (gloss)

Preparation

■ If necessary, remove any hinges
    and paint the toy box – inside
    and out – with broken white.
    Allow to dry.
■ If you are using an old wooden
    chest, fill any blemishes with wood
    filler. Allow to dry and sand
    the entire toy box with 400-grit
    sandpaper. Paint as above.

1 Apply 4 coats of Polvin Lemon Ice, inside and out, allowing time to dry in between coats. We used a sponge roller which gives a more textured finish than a normal paintbrush.

2 Make a mixture of 1 part white Polvin, 2 parts acrylic scumble glaze and 3 parts water. Using a crumpled nappy liner, dab the white over the yellow. This softens the colour and gives an attractive two-tone colour effect. The paint effect is only applied to the outside of the box.

3 Mix 2 parts yellow ochre and 1 part raw umber with a little scumble glaze (enough to achieve the consistency of thick pouring cream). Paint the edges and ridges of the toy box to create a contrasting effect, using a small paintbrush – at least 2 coats are required. When dry, rub the white paint mix over with a nappy liner to soften the colour.

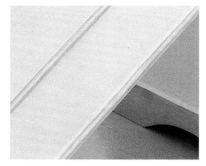

4 Apply a coat of Modge Podge over the entire outside surface of the toy box. Arrange your Wallies in position by using the temporary sticking dots provided in the pack. If you're using cut-outs, position them with Prestik and lightly mark their positions with a soft pencil.

5 Remove the Wallies one at a time and moisten the back with a wet sponge for 5 seconds, ensuring that the edges have been moistened. Smooth back on gently with a roller, working over a damp nappy liner. Dab away any excess water and leave to dry. If you're using cut-outs, glue down as discussed on page 49.

6 Apply one coat of Modge Podge only over the areas where you have glued the Wallies. Complete by applying 6 coats of Woodcare Ultra Varnish to the entire toy box, waiting 24 hours in between coats for drying. Sand gently after each coat using 600-grit sandpaper. Don't sand after the final coat!

BELOW *Motifs such as these fairies are sure to delight any little girl aspiring to be a fairy princess. You can use the solid block as is, with individual cut-outs added from the scattered motifs to form your own unique design.*

Christmas

Bearing in mind the increasing cost of Christmas decorating, we have decided to include this chapter to give you some ideas on attractive yet inexpensive ways of making decorations, special Christmas packaging and presentation boxes. The boxes can be used purely as decorative pieces under the tree or as gift presentation boxes.

It is also a good idea to decoupage a galvanized steel bucket and use that year after year to stand your Christmas tree in.

RIGHT *We used the wrapping paper for the red and the white Christmas balls, first painting the paper with metallic gold paint to enhance the colour of the stars. This was followed by a coat of Modge Podge before the stars were cut out.*

We painted one ball with red metallic paint before gluing on the stars, while the other was left white. The third ball was also painted with metallic red paint, then covered with gold size, leaving gaps for the red paint to show through, and decorated with gold leaf (see page 105).

You can also decorate these polystyrene balls with stickers in a Christmas theme. These are widely available from most stationery and craft shops.

OPPOSITE PAGE *Christmas bags, special presentation boxes, and Christmas candles are discussed on pages 104-107.*

Christmas tree decorations

We have painted and decorated polystyrene balls for our Christmas tree decorations. They are cheap and fun to make and we've gold leafed some of the balls to give a more vibrant finish than you will be able to achieve by simply painting the balls. You can personalize these decorations by making one for every member of the family — apply the names with lettraset.

Polystyrene balls are obtainable from craft shops and cross-stitch outlets. These shops also have stars, bells and other small objects in polystyrene. Decoupage these for variation.

A threading needle, obtainable from craft shops, is used to draw the gold thread through the ball (it looks like a long crochet hook). Using gold thread will give your decorations a professional finish.

ABOVE *The Santa Clause images on these bags were taken from one sheet of wrapping paper, as was the holly, which involved a lot of intricate cutting. Sections of holly were cut out and then joined together to form the borders.*

Candles and bags

We made transfers for the candles, as it is easier to mould these around the candles. When using transfers on candles, they don't stick when they are wet because of the wax.

Glue the transfers on with white glue. Wipe away the excess glue and leave to dry. Candles cannot be varnished since the varnish will burn. The candles will be used anyway, so they don't have to be as durable as other decoupaged items.

Plain-paper bags can be decorated with cut-outs and left-over gold leaf flakes. A decoupaged bag is a very impressive and personalised way of presenting a gift. For these bags, we used transparent paper glue to stick down the Santa Clause cut-outs.

We then gold-leafed the handles, and applied gold size haphazardly to the areas surrounding the cut-out and sprinkled them with gold-leaf flakes. When the areas in between the flakes remained sticky even after two days, we didn't want to wait any longer for the gold size to dry.

We took a chance and sealed the bags, including the handles, with hard varnish, even though you're only sup-posed to use shellac on gold leaf. Up until now, three months later, the bags are still okay (although oxidiza-tion could still take place).

The stickiness also disappeared once the varnish dried. But bear in mind that the only time you can apply varnish over a sticky surface, is when you work with gold size.

Quick and easy method of gold leafing (gilding)

Gold leaf can be used almost everywhere to add sparkle to your decoupaged items – on the routed edges of boxes, the rim of a plate, or in flake form, sprinkled over a painted surface, as we did for the gift bags. The metal leaf is brighter and more vibrant than any gold paint that you can buy, and does not fade.

True gold leaf is very expensive and difficult to obtain. You can achieve basically the same look by using the cheaper alternative, known as Dutch metal or metal leaf. The metal leaf is sold in booklet form with protective paper between each leaf. You will also need Wunder size (gold size), which is the glue required for adhesion of the metal leaf, as well as shellac and white spirits for sealing.

- Paint the surface to be leafed with acrylic paint of your choice. Use either the same colour as the rest of your item, or a traditional gilding base colour (red oxide or black). Leave to dry.
- Using an artists' brush, apply 1 coat of gold size to the area to be gilded. Leave for about 15 minutes until it becomes sticky.
- Before handling the metal leaf, apply a light dusting of talcum powder to your hands to prevent it from dis-colouring, as perspiration from your hands can cause oxidization.
- Cut the metal leaf (with the protective sheets covering it) into either strips or squares, depending on the shape of the item you are covering, and lay it over the sticky gold size. Once the metal leaf has touched the gold size, it will stick and you will not be able to reposition it.
- Make sure that your hands are covered in powder and gently press the leaf into place. You could also rub it into place using a soft cloth. Leave for approximately one hour to set.
- Using a soft brush, gently brush off the loose bits – save them in an envelope for future use – and polish with a soft cloth to get rid of all excess flakes.
- Seal areas that have been gold-leafed with a coat of shellac. This comes in flake form and can only be used once it has been mixed with white spirits. The rest of the decoupaged item should be sealed with any suit-able varnish.
- We did not seal the polystyrene balls because poly-styrene sometimes reacts with varnish when gold leaf is involved. As they wouldn't be handled much, we decided that sealing wasn't necessary.

Boxes of all shapes and sizes

Christmas is a good time to make lots of decoupage boxes. These boxes could be used to serve nuts and chocolates when guests arrive, or as gift boxes filled with edible delights or jewellery. Even an empty box will be appreciated!

Give them gold edges and use a gold-filled Antique Crackle finish to give them a rich, classic Christmas look. Bear in mind that it takes at least 6 coats of gold paint to give a vibrant, gold leaf-like finish.

The edges of the tray above were finished with metal-leaf, which is more vibrant than gold paint.

The images on the tray came from the same wrapping paper that was used for the bags on page 104. For variation, the border framing santa was cut away for the bags, but left in position for the tray. The fine details were carefully cut out after sealing with Modge Podge.

We were lucky to find the wrapping paper for the white and gold boxes as it tied in perfectly with our colour scheme. The gold is really vibrant, like gold leaf, so no gold trim was needed. After applying Modge Podge to the paper, we covered the boxes completely and sealed them with 3 coats of hard varnish.

OPPOSITE PAGE *We used only 6 coats of varnish for these boxes, which will provide more than enough protection for an item used only once a year.*

List of suppliers

Y ou should find all the products needed to create beautiful decoupage from your local hardware store and craft shop. If you find it difficult to obtain any product, please consult this list of suppliers. Many of these suppliers offer a mail-order service and will gladly arrange for products to be forwarded to wherever you are. Details such as telephone numbers and addresses were correct at the time of going to print (April 2001).

Crafty Supplies
The Atrium
Main Road
CLAREMONT
Tel: 021 671 0286
Fax: 021 671 0308

The dotty dog
Pick 'n Pay Centre
TOKAI
Tel: 021 712 3923

The Hearth & Home Shop
Unit E7
Access Park
KENILWORTH
Tel: 021 683 1149

Kidz-a-Peal
Pick 'n Pay Centre
Gabriel Road
PLUMSTEAD
Tel: 021 762 3543

Cape Arts & Crafts
8 Falmingo Square
Blaauberg Road
TABLE VIEW
Tel: 021 556 1150

Crafty Friends
Shop 10
Old Bellville Jail
Tygervalley Road
BELLVILLE
Tel: 021 914 0257

Articles
290B Main Road
PAARL
Tel: 021 871 1493
Fax: 021 871 1494

Whale Rock Mica
2 Harbour Road
HERMANUS
Tel: 028 312 4254

Basketcase
Marklaan Centre
GEORGE
Tel: 044 874 4748
Cell: 0836253945

Decouden
Ou Fabriek
Main Road
KNYSNA
Tel: 044 3820317

Metelerkamp's Mica
Waterfront Drive
KNYSNA
Tel: 044 382 5388
Fax: 044 382 3019

C-View Hardware
Florina Place
Main Street
PLETTENBERG BAY
Tel: 044 533 4460

Aneen's Florist & Craft Centre
97 Heugh Road
Walmer
PORT ELIZABETH
Tel: 041 581 7504

Crafty Arts
Walmer Park
Main Street
Walmer
PORT ELIZABETH
Tel: 041 794 7000

House of Arts
Shop 5 Ninth Avenue Centre
Main Street
Walmer
PORT ELIZABETH
Cell: 0828668860

D & A Mica Hardware
34 Bathurst Street
GRAHAMSTOWN
Tel: 046 622 7301

Paint Unique
3 Dersley Street
Nahoon
EAST LONDON
Tel: 043 735 4345

Spectra Upfront
32 Bushell Street
QUEENSTOWN
Tel: 045 858 1873
Fax: 045 839 2356

L & P Stationers
College Square
10 Zastron Street
BLOEMFONTEIN
Tel: 051 430 8608

Westdene Hardware
Cor Zastron & 2nd Avenue
WESTDENE
Tel: 051 447 6881

Ficksburg Dock Mica
69 Fontein Street
FICKSBURG
Tel: 051 933 4908

Krafters
Shop 7
Pick 'n Pay Centre
Bok Street
WELKOM
Tel: 057 352 4186

Village Arts & Crafts
7 Bruwer Street
BETHLEHEM
Tel: 058 303 3714

Kroonstad Kuns Sentrum
16 Hill Street
KROONSTAD
Tel: 056 212 3423

Art Mates
Shop 303 Musgrave Centre
DURBAN
Tel: 031 2010094

Bluff Mica
Shop 28
Pick 'n Pay Shopping Centre
Bluff
DURBAN
Tel: 031 467 4147

Cottage Craft
Shop 2
Hillcrest Shopping Centre
Old Main Road
Hillcrest
DURBAN
Tel: 031 765 1095

Artwise
Shop 337
Sanlam Centre
PINETOWN
Tel: 031 701 1824

His & Hers Hardware
111 Marine Drive
MARGATE
Tel: 039 312 1174

Roy's Mica Hardware
Shop 201
Sanlam Centre
Biyela Street
EMPANGENI
Tel: 035 772 7760

Art Shop
The Wembley Centre
60 Commercial Road
PIETERMARITZBURG
Tel: 033 394 7917

Hayfields Dock Hardware
Shop 54
Hayfields Mall
Scottsville
PIETERMARITZBURG
Tel: 033 386 2464

Brooklyn Crafts
Brooklyn Wool Shop
Shop 481A
Vatlika Centre
Sehrsen Street
PRETORIA
Tel: 012 460 4504

Maridadi Crafts
Centurion Boulevard Centre
CENTURION
Tel: 012 663 4030

Schweickerdt Art Centre & Gallery
351 Lynnwood Road
MENLO PARK
Tel: 012 4605406

Barney's Westgate
Westgate Shopping Centre
ROODEPOORT
Tel: 011 768 0880

Barneys Blackheath
One Mimosa
D F Malan Drive
Blackheath
JOHANNESBURG
Tel: 011 478 2686

Country Crafts
12 Apiesdoring Ave
RANDPARK RIDGE EXT 1
Tel: 011 792 8067
Fax: 011 792 8188

Herbert Evans Art Shop
Galleria Centre
ROSEBANK
Tel: 011 447 3262
Fax: 011 447 4146

Town & Country
Unit 8
No 31 6th Street
Wynberg
JOHANNESBURG
Tel: 011 786 1193

Hobart House
Hobart Shopping Centre
Bryanston
JOHANNESBURG
Tel: 011 706 4471

Barneys Fourways
4 Ways Mall
Bryanston
JOHANNESBURG
Tel: 011 465 6490

Brasch Hobby Manufacturers &
Distributors of Heritage Products
For Trade Enquires
Tel: 011 493 9100
Fax: 011 493 2860

Colonial Green
Shop 6 Mutual Mews
Rivonia Boulevard
JOHANNESBURG
Tel: 011 803 1035

The Hearth & Home Shop
Shop 52
Honeydew Shopping Centre
JOHANNESBURG
Tel: 011 795 4015
Fax: 011 795 3345

Decoupage & Craft Centre
Shop 3A
Club House Centre
Ferndale
JOHANNESBURG
Tel: 011 791 6920
Cell: 0832536229

Tool & Garden Centre
14 8th Avenue
Northmead
JOHANNESBURG
Tel: 011 849 6931

Meyersdal Mica
Shop 31
Meyersdal Mall
MEYERSDAL
Tel: 011 867 5206

Bedfordview Mica Hardware
Shop 17
Village View
Van Buuren Road
Bedfordview
JOHANNESBURG
Tel: 011 455 1007

Eastgate Mica Hardware
Eastgate Shopping Centre
BEDFORDVIEW
Tel: 011 616 4129

Famili Krafts
18 Heron Drive
Three Rivers East
VEREENIGING
Tel: 016 423 6734
Fax: 016 423 6734

Art & Craft Studio
17 Kruger Road
VEREENIGING
Tel: 016 422 3215

Heimberg Mica Hardware
Pick 'n Pay Centre
POTCHEFSTROOM
Tel: 018 294 7423

Jacks Paint Germiston
Cor George & Meyer Streets
GERMISTON
Tel: 011 873 4640

Piet Retief Mica Hardware
34A Mark Street
PIET RETIEF
Tel: 017 826 0799

Tip Top Mica Hardware
18A Krogh Street
STANDERTON
Tel: 017 712 2472

Northmead Dock Mica
Northmead Square
O' Reilly Merry Street
Benoni
Tel: 011 425 6853

Trish's Crafts
Parkrand Centre
Van Wyk Louw Ave
Parkrand
BOKSBURG
Tel: 011 913 1789
Cell: 0824524029

Middelburg Mica Hardware
Mica Centre
Cor Laver & Church Streets
MIDDELBURG
Tel: 013 282 8642

Book 'n Pen
58A Hendrik Verwoerd Street
NIGEL
Tel: 011 814 2734

Stitchcraft
104 KaMkholo Building
Voortrekker Street
NELSPRUIT
Tel: 013 752 3441

Burgers Mica Hardware
6 Eeufees Street
BETHAL
Tel: 017 647 6608

Hobby Horse
Shop 2
The Arcade
Roon Street
SWAKOPMUND NAMIBIA
Tel: 09264 64 402875

Jenny's Place
78 Sam Nujoma Road
WINDHOEK NAMIBIA
Tel: +09264 61 236792
Fax: +09264 61 2255408